NATIONAL PARKS OF THE WEST

NATIONAL PARKS of the WEST

By the Editors of Sunset Books
and Sunset Magazine

Lane Magazine & Book Company
Menlo Park, California

SUPERVISING EDITORS: PAUL C. JOHNSON, JACK McDOWELL

TRAVEL EDITOR OF SUNSET MAGAZINE: LARRY SMITH

TECHNICAL CONSULTANT: Dorr Yeager, Former Regional Chief
of Interpretation, National Park Service

BOOK DESIGN CONSULTANTS: Adrian Wilson, Richard S. Coyne

GRAPHICS COORDINATION AND LAYOUT: Judith Whipple

MAPS: James M. Cutter, Doris Marsh

ILLUSTRATIONS: Earl Thollander, E. D. Bills

Executive Editor, Sunset Books: David E. Clark

This book was lithographed by Peninsula Lithograph Co., Menlo Park, using
film prepared by Balzer-Shopes, San Francisco, and bound by Cardoza
Bookbinding Co., San Francisco. Body type is Monotype Bell 402 composed
by Holmes Typography, Inc., San Jose, California. Type for headings is
Dimensia. Paper for body is Mountie Enamel furnished by Northwest Paper
Co., Cloquet, Minnesota.

Title Page photo: Cascade Pass, North Cascades National Park, by Ansel Adams.
Front Cover: Yosemite Falls, Yosemite National Park, by David Muench.
Back Cover: Rocky Mountain Bighorn sheep, Glacier National Park, by Don Wright.

PREFACE

THIS BOOK IS A PICTORIAL INTERPRETATION of the national parks in the west, the score of scenic preserves whose very names are household synonyms for spectacular beauty—Yellowstone, Yosemite, Grand Canyon, Zion, Mount McKinley, Olympic—parks that encompass within their 12 million acres most of the nation's finest mountain and desert scenery.

As its title indicates, this is a book about *national parks*, which are defined as areas of outstanding scenic beauty that have been set aside by Congress to be preserved in their natural state for the benefit and enjoyment of the people. Although some *national monuments* partially meet this definition, and all of them are operated by the National Park Service, we have reluctantly omitted them for lack of space (there are 63 within the geographical scope of this book) and have confined our coverage to the 22 areas officially designated as national parks.

This edition is a second look at the subject, necessitated by the innumerable changes that have taken place within the parks in the half decade since this book was first published. New roads have been built, old routes re-aligned, and miles of trail added. Off-season facilities have been developed, concessioners have upgraded and expanded their facilities, and, most important, Congress has added three new Western parks to the roster. All in all, the changes have been significant and numerous and are here reflected in this revision, issued as the parks start their second century.

We wish to acknowledge with appreciation the excellent cooperation that we received from the concessioners and from the National Park Service, from Washington down to the individual parks, in the supplying and checking of technical information for this book. We would like to thank particularly the superintendents and ranger naturalists who worked with us—absolving them of any responsibility for errors of fact or interpretation that may have crept into the book.

Our pictorial interpretation of the parks is offered with the wish that it may partly accomplish what John Muir hoped his own book on the national parks would do when it was published in 1898. Like Muir, we have tried "to show forth the beauty, grandeur, and all-embracing usefulness of our wild mountain forest reservations and parks, with a view to inciting people to come and enjoy them, and get them into their hearts, that so at length their preservation and right use might be made sure of."

CONTENTS

THE NATIONAL PARK IDEA

"THOUSANDS OF TIRED, NERVE-SHAKEN, OVER-CIVILIZED people are beginning to find out that going to the mountains is going home; that wildness is a necessity; and that mountain parks and reservations are useful not only as fountains of timber and irrigating rivers, but as fountains of life." So wrote John Muir, naturalist, conservationist, and pioneer spokesman for the national parks.

When Muir expressed these sentiments, the year was 1898. There were only four national parks in existence—three of them in California—and they could be reached only by an endless stage ride over backbreaking roads. The fact that thousands were making this arduous trip is an indication of the depth of the need that was felt even then to "go home to the mountains."

What Muir sensed as a significant truth then is even more cogent today, as 24 million visitors converge each year on the Western national parks, seeking spiritual and physical renewal and the reassurance of contact, however brief and communal, with nature.

Westerners are fortunate to have within their domain the lion's share of the nation's spectacular scenery, and most of it is contained within the boundaries of the national parks lying west of the Continental Divide. Here, held in trust for the country as a whole are a dozen scenic superlatives—the deepest canyons, highest waterfalls, tallest peaks, and biggest trees in the nation. Here the traveler can stand witness to the awesome forces of earthbuilding: the power of running water or grinding ice to shape the surface of the earth; the restlessness pent up within the planet, revealed in fire-fountains of lava or spouting columns of steam. He can observe the grand cycle of life, seen in the wash of spring wildflowers, the frolicking bear cubs, or the golden fires of October aspen. In a few weeks' travel, a vacationer can see perpetual snow and active glaciers,

SERENE AND TIMELESS, *the soaring redwoods remind man of his origins, inspire him with their beauty, reassure him with their will to live. To preserve scenic wonders such as these for all men to enjoy is the dedicated mission of the National Park Service.*

ANSEL ADAMS

9

petrified forests and mountains of glass; he can follow a trail through a wild-flower park, watch armies of elk on the move, or walk through a dead city that was a vital community 1,500 years before Plymouth Rock. Within the parks, motorists can drive over the spine of a continent, and hikers can safely roam for weeks in a primeval wilderness, unchanged from the days of the cavemen.

To devotees of the national parks, it is often things subtler than geysers, fumaroles, and the riven earth that bring them back vacation after vacation. To the camper, it is the camaraderie of the campfire or the trail; to the fisherman the park is a place where time stands still while he trolls a lake or casts into a rushing stream. To families it is a place where the flash of wonder and delight glows on the faces of their children when they first feel a running stream against their shins, or see a fawn, a thieving jay or chipmunk, or Smokey in all his natural majesty. To some, it is a garden of trees and wildflowers, stones and lichens; an aviary; and a place to watch animals going about their daily chores. To all, the parks offer the soul-stretching experience of being alone in a world of wide-open space, of grand vistas of forest and mountain and great storms rumbling across the land. The experience is remembered for the tang of fresh mountain air, the blessing of pure silence, the benediction of alpenglow. In short, the parks offer a return to nature, and the renewal that comes from re-contact with a wild and primitive environment.

To make sure that all who want to enjoy the parks can do so, at whatever level of experience, is the dedicated mission of the National Park Service.

The seed of the national park idea was planted more than a century ago in California, where commercial exploitation of Yosemite Valley and the senseless cutting of giant sequoias had aroused great public concern. A handful of men banded together to put pressure on Congress to preserve the beautiful valley and a grove of the irreplaceable trees, both of which were on federal property. With little debate, a law was passed in 1864 and signed by President Lincoln, then in the heat of the Civil War, that granted Yosemite Valley and the Mariposa Grove

TO A CHILD, A NATIONAL PARK *may be remembered as the place where she first saw wild creatures going about their daily chores, or where, specifically, she fed half a sandwich to an ill-tempered marmot named Freddie.*

of Big Trees to the state of California. This was the first time that any government anywhere had set aside public lands purely for the preservation of scenic values, and, as such, the law was a landmark in conservation.

The portion of Yosemite turned over to the state was only a 10-square-mile strip that included the famous valley and a square mile of trees 35 miles to the south. In size, it was far from the huge park of today. Furthermore, as a grant to a state, this was not a "national" park in today's meaning of the term, but a state park. The first true national park was created in Yellowstone eight years later, and it is from it that the National Park Service dates its official beginning.

The idea for a national park was first presented before an historic campfire in 1870 by a Montana attorney named Cornelius Hedges. He was a member of a famous exploring party known as the Washburn-Langford-Doane expedition that surveyed the wonders of Yellowstone (see page 217) with the purpose of puncturing or confirming the incredible rumors then circulating about the thermal spectacles in the area.

After exploring the region for more than a month, on their last night before returning home, the party held a campfire meeting at the junction of three rivers in western Yellowstone. Under the laws of the day, all were entitled to stake claims on the land and its geysers. As the men were discussing how they would divide this wonderland among themselves, Hedges made a far-reaching proposal. Turning the conversation away from private gain, he eloquently proposed that they work for the preservation of the whole area under government protection. The men enthusiastically endorsed the idea (all but one hold-out), and after their return, several of them campaigned for a law to set aside the area. So effective was their presentation that Congress passed the necessary legislation only 17 months after the expedition's return, thus creating the first, and as far as anyone then knew the last, national park.

The law, based in part on the earlier legislation that had created the Yosemite Grant, set forth principles that have been followed with some modifications for a century. Under this legislative mandate, the National Park Service is charged with a dual responsibility: (a) to preserve for all time the natural wonders within its boundaries in an undisturbed state and (b) to make them available for the enjoyment of all the people.

Under its commitment to preserve the parks in their natural state, the Park Service is required to protect wildlife from trappers and hunters and to preserve the forests, streams, and lakes from despoliation. Thus, timber cutting is prohibited and trees are left to topple of old age or to be blown down in a windstorm. Once fallen, they are left where they fell. Mining and extraction of petroleum are forbidden, and so is the grazing of sheep and cattle. Private cabins cannot be built within a national park, and the only structures permitted are those needed by government services and the concessioners.

To promote understanding of the natural wonders within their borders, the parks provide museums, visitor centers, booklets, and indestructible roadside labels for every prominent feature. Ranger naturalists, many of them "90-day

Two great conservationists, *President Theodore Roosevelt and John Muir, stand on Glacier Point in Yosemite, where they camped together for 5 days in 1903. As a result of this meeting, Roosevelt returned to Washington determined to expand the federal protection of the nation's scenic, historic, and natural heritage. In the next few years, he brought protection to several million acres by proclaiming national monuments.*

wonders" (summer recruits largely from the teaching profession), give interpretive lectures and conduct nature walks, ranging from a gentle stroll around a lily pond to a stiff, full-day hike up a glacier and back.

To make the parks accessible to everyone, the Park System builds and maintains roads and trails and assures food, housing, and services by granting long-term concessions to corporations, usually only one or two to a park. Such concessions are closely supervised by the Service (and to a certain extent, by Congress) and are largely staffed by eager college students, who earn paid vacations by working for the summer as a "savage," "heaver," or "bubble queen."

Preservation of the natural scene by the Park Service so that all the people may enjoy it often calls for skillful balancing of opposing needs.

Under its charter, the Park Service must welcome all who wish to come to the parks. With improved roads and the proliferation of the automobile, the parks have become more accessible to more people each year, and crowded conditions prevail in seasons of heavy tourist travel. Yellowstone clocks 1,000 cars an hour on its east-west highway, Yosemite checks in 45,000 visitors over a Fourth of

July weekend, and in both parks the tourists head instinctively for the centers of popular interest, thereby compounding congestion. Although the Park Service tries to interest tourists in outlying areas and encourages off-season visits, these measures do not solve the problem. Crowding increases each year, threatening to submerge the parks, scenic wonders and all.

And what of the future? Tradition and legal precedent do not guarantee that the natural parks can be kept to their dedicated mission without vigilant adherence to the policies under which they are operated.

It is theoretically possible to create a new national park anywhere within the federal domain today, but in areas containing mineral deposits, harvestable timber, dam sites, or grazing land, opposition is almost inevitable. One of the newest parks, Canyonlands, located in a mineral-rich area of Utah, was long a subject of controversy and was much shrunk in size from earlier proposals when it was finally approved. And it is not surprising that national parks recently established in Washington's North Cascades and in California's coast-redwood belt were vigorously opposed, not only by timber industry advocates but by spokesmen for communities dependent on the lumbering industry.

Even after a new park has been established by Congress, its existence is not fully secure until all the needed land has been purchased. Unfortunately, land values usually move faster than Congress, and the initial appropriations passed are often less than adequate at the start and are soon left behind by spiraling real estate prices. Thus, Point Reyes National Seashore, welcomed with fanfare to the roster of federal preserves in 1962, has been almost crippled by lack of funds to purchase land originally earmarked for the park. Redwood National Park, a patchwork-quilt of state and federal lands, is deeply embroiled in land-swapping and other financial complexities that may simmer for years before the park is finally consolidated.

For that matter, long-established parks are never completely immune from forays by mineral, water, and recreational interests seeking to exploit the public domain. The constituted agencies are sometimes ill equipped to repel invaders because of red tape, interservice rivalries, or local pressures, and occasionally have to rely on bolstering from the outside to protect the public's scenic heritage. Conservationists have leaped to the barricade several times in recent years and their task forces are on permanent alert. In the forefront of the defending forces, the bristly Sierra Club has employed every strategem—court injunctions, lawsuits, advertising campaigns—to keep parklands inviolate. The club has fought to prevent Grand Canyon from being dammed into a lake, to block highway engineers from bulldozing a swath through public groves of redwoods, to stop developers from cutting a highway through Sequoia National Park. Conservationists win some of the battles, compromise most of them, and lose a few. But the struggle continues for the protectors both within and outside the guardian agencies, for there will always be men who can see trees only as lumber, rivers as sources of energy, canyons as reservoirs, and mountain meadows as beef in the supermarket, heedless of the broader values of the natural landscape to the nation as a whole.

MOUNT McKINLEY

HOME OF THE INVISIBLE MOUNTAIN

PARK FACTS: *Location*: South central Alaska. *Discovered*: 1896. *Established*: February 26, 1917. *Size*: 3,030 sq. mi. *Altitude*: 1,400-20,320 feet. *Climate*: Cool, wet, and windy; temperatures—50° to 80°. *Season*: June 1 to September 15. *Visitors in 1969*: 45,500.

MOUNT McKINLEY, THE HIGHEST MOUNTAIN IN NORTH AMERICA, lies only 250 miles south of the Arctic Circle. Guarding the Alaska Range with its neighbor Mount Foraker, this great peak rises to the sublime height of 20,320 feet. Small wonder the Indians of the region called it *Denali* (The High One).

Mount McKinley National Park is one of America's largest parks, and in its 3,030 square miles man has intruded but slightly. There is only one road and one area of major development.

Long before you reach the park, you can see the glacier-mantled mountain, stark and forboding, a giant among giants. The first glimpse from the highway is at a point 8 miles from McKinley Park Station, but the mountain does not appear in its full glory until the last 25 or 30 miles. The views are less obstructed here, and although the summit is still 20 miles from the road at its nearest point, it appears so near that one is sure a 10-minute walk should bring him to the snowy slopes. Unfortunately, it is not visible from the hotel.

Probably the best view, and certainly the most photographed, is from near the end of the road, with Wonder Lake in the foreground. Mount McKinley is a stunning sight at midday, when the sunlight glistens on its snow and glaciers, but at sunrise or during the long subarctic twilight it is magnificent. Then delicate pastel shades enshroud it, changing with every shift of light, softening and transforming it from a great mass of granite, ice, and snow into a thing of ethereal beauty.

Weather is the enemy of visitors to this park. Summers are cool and windy, and you can count on rain half the time. You can be in the area for days and never see the mountain at all because of low-hanging clouds. Yet, even when

"THE HIGH ONE," highest peak on the North American continent, Mount McKinley rises 20,320 feet above sea level, dominates a great wilderness province 250 miles south of the Arctic Circle.

ANSEL ADAMS

15

the mountain is not visible, there is much else of interest. The park is a sanctuary for wildlife, and you can see many animals from the road, especially if you drive slowly, park frequently, and use field glasses.

The mighty Toklat grizzly is frequently seen. Moose are common and are usually seen browsing in willow thickets. But the greatest wildlife show is provided by the barren-ground caribou, close relative of the domesticated reindeer. The annual migratory route of these animals crosses the park, and for a few days in late June and early July hundreds can be seen moving leisurely over the slopes and along the river bottoms. It is difficult to determine exactly when the migration will occur, and you can count yourself extremely fortunate if you are in the right place during the short time it is visible from the road.

Most of the park lies above timberline. In this northern latitude timberline ranges between 2,500 and 3,000 feet. Alpine tundra, not to be confused with arctic tundra, covers much of the park. It is of two types, wet and dry. Wet tundra is characterized by a luxuriant growth of grasses, mosses, lichens, and low shrubs. Small ponds frequently dot this dense mat, and hiking is difficult. Dry tundra is typical of higher, well-drained soils, but it is composed of dwarf plant forms.

The park road varies in elevation from 1,600 feet at the entrance to about 4,000 feet near Eielson Visitor Center. Most of the roads are gravel, although a few sections are asphalt surface. The road is hilly and winding, with frequent vistas and parking areas for viewing wildlife. Ordinarily it is open from June 1 to September 15. Campgrounds with fireplaces and water are conveniently spaced along the road. Wood should be obtained before entering the park.

Considering its isolation, Mount McKinley National Park is surprisingly accessible. During the summer the Alaska Railroad takes passengers daily almost to the door of the hotel. The Denali Highway, open from about June 1 to September 15, serves the park and connects with the Richardson Highway at Paxson, 160 miles from the entrance.

The park was established in 1917 primarily to protect wildlife from extinction by an army of hunters that was expected to arrive when the Alaska Railroad was completed to the area. Conservation groups, such as the Boone and Crockett Club of New York and the Campfire Club of America, worked under the leadership of the "Father of McKinley Park," Charles Sheldon, to persuade Congress to establish the park, which it did six years before the rails reached it.

Another reason for creating the park was to establish a reserve around the largest mountain on the continent. The "High One," known to explorers and prospectors for a century, was officially named in 1897 for President McKinley by a prospector named W. A. Dickey, who bestowed the name in a fit of exasperation. After spending several weary days listening to a pair of fellow prospectors advance arguments in favor of free silver, he chose in retaliation to name the peak for the leading advocate of the gold standard.

TYPICAL OF THE LAKES *that abound in the wilderness around Mount McKinley is Deneki on the outer edge of the park, just off the Denali Highway. It is a favorite haunt of moose and waterfowl.*

MOUNT MCKINLEY **17**

THREE GLACIERS FLOW TOGETHER *to form a single massive ice sheet in the southwestern corner of the park. The dark ribbons are deposits of rock (medial moraines) carried by the advancing ice. The scalloped ice (ogives) is thought to be some sort of an annual ring. The extreme range of elevation within the park—from 1,400 to 20,320 feet—provides both the altitude to form, and the slope to move glacial ice.*

SUDDEN STORMS AND
TREACHEROUS ICE *make the ascent
of Mt. McKinley a risky
venture. Many climbers
have reached the summit since it
was first conquered in 1913;
some have died in making the
attempt. Parties ranging from
poorly equipped amateurs to
elaborately outfitted expeditions
have climbed it to study weather
and cosmic rays, field-test
cold-weather food and gear for
the army, retrieve bodies from a
crashed military transport plane,
or, simply, to conquer the
continent's highest mountain.*

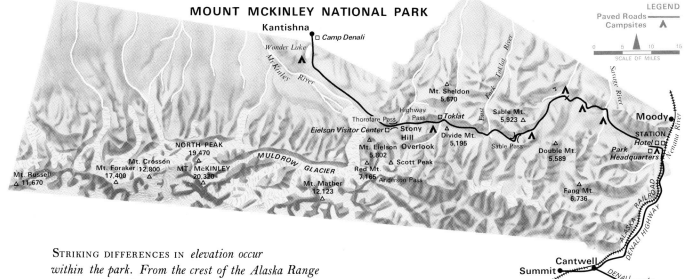

MOUNT McKINLEY NATIONAL PARK

LEGEND
Paved Roads
Campsites ▲

0   5   10   15
SCALE OF MILES

Kantishna
□ Camp Denali

Wonder Lake

McKinley River

Mt. Sheldon
5,670

Highway Pass
□ Toklat

Thorofare Pass

Eielson Visitor Center □   Stony Hill

Sable Mt.
5,923

East Fork   Toklat River   Savage River

Moody ●

STATION
Hotel □□

NORTH PEAK
19,470
△

Mt. Crosson
12,800

MULDROW GLACIER

Mt. Eleson
5,802

Divide Mt.
5,195

Sable Pass

Park
Headquarters

Mt. Foraker
17,400

MT. McKINLEY
20,320

Scott Peak

Double Mt.
5,589

Mt. Russell
△ 11,670

Mt. Mather
12,123

Red Mt.
7,165   Anderson Pass

Fang Mt.
6,736

ALASKA RAILROAD   DENALI HIGHWAY   Nenana River

Cantwell
Summit ●

DENALI HIGHWAY
to Paxson,
156 miles

STRIKING DIFFERENCES IN *elevation occur
within the park. From the crest of the Alaska Range
to the tundra below is an 18,000-foot drop.*

MOUNT McKINLEY   **19**

ONE OF THE MOST INCREDIBLE SIGHTS *in the park is the annual migration of the caribou in great herds, sometimes numbering as many as 5,000 animals. The herds travel slowly on a broad front, leaving behind scores of parallel trails only a few feet apart. They follow general route patterns within a region 200 to 300 miles in diameter, traveling several hundred miles in their annual circuit. They winter outside the park and return to it in spring for two or three months before moving out again. Caribou feed on lichen, and their wide-ranging migration keeps it from being over-grazed.*

CHARLES J. OTT

GINNY HILL WOOD

EXCELLENT SWIMMERS, *moose spend a great deal of time wading and swimming in ponds in search of aquatic plants, a source of summer food, and escaping the torment of the insects that plague them. Moose can graze as easily under water as in a meadow. The great antlers are grown annually and only by the males. The moose is the largest member of the deer family*

CHARLES J. OTT
RICHARD PRASIL

RED FOX PUP (LEFT), *grooming himself in his burrow opening, stays close to shelter to escape his natural enemies. Foxes live off mice, squirrels, rabbits, and ptarmigan* (RIGHT), *a plump bird that changes to white in winter.*

UNIQUE AMONG McKINLEY NATIVES *are the Dall sheep that roam in bands over the higher slopes. At home on slippery talus they are relatively safe on steep slopes from attack by less-sure-footed predators.*

COMMON THROUGHOUT THE PARK, *grizzlies are best viewed at a respectful distance. The big, hump-shouldered beasts appear in a range of coloring, from blond to cinnamon brown. The species was once common from Mexico to Alaska, but has been exterminated over much of its original range and may only be seen in the United States in McKinley, Glacier, and Yellowstone parks. These powerful wild animals present a potential hazard to back-country hikers and wildlife photographers.*
Visitors to the park are advised to contact the park personnel for safety instructions before venturing too far away from the resort area.

NORTH CASCADES

AMERICA'S ALPINE WILDERNESS

PARK FACTS: *Location:* North central Washington. *Discovered:* 1792 by Captain Vancouver. *Established:* Oct. 2, 1968. *Size:* 1,053 square miles, including Ross Lake and Lake Chelan national recreation areas. *Altitude:* Sea level to 9,000 feet. *Climate:* Cool and damp on west side of Cascades; warm days, cool nights on east side. *Season:* Early April to mid-Oct.; high country mid-June to mid-Sept. *Visitors, 1969:* 360,000.

A LAND FOR MOUNTAINEERS, North Cascades reveals its grandeur and its trailside surprises only to those who frequent its hiking or riding trails. Travelers can approach the perimeter of the park by automobile or boat, or can be flown to Lake Chelan or Ross Lake, but may not land within the boundaries of the National Park.

A few miles of resolute trudging brings spectacular individual rewards. Everywhere is the looming presence of the mountains, with soaring glacier-burdened peaks, cloud-piercing needle spires, flower-starred ridgetop meadows, clumps of alpine fir, and views down steep heather slopes to mounded gray moraines and the deep, wooded, glacial valleys beyond. There are the deep crackling sounds of sloughing ice and tumbling avalanches when the day is warm, and of thunder when it is stormy; and always there is a background roar of falling water, sometimes muted by distance, sometimes lost in the rush of the wind, accented by the chirp of a pika, or accompanied by the summery hum of a fly.

For travelers who are not inured to the damp weather of northern Washington, a trip into this realm can have its disappointments. Summer weather on the western slopes is normally wet—meaning rain, hail, snow, sleet, envelopment in dripping clouds, or simply the lingering presence of leaden overcast that keeps wet things (including the hiker himself) from drying out. Often, vacationers in the park will sense rather than see the surrounding mountains from one day to the next. However, experienced hikers equip themselves with appropriate rain gear and tolerate the drizzle in the knowledge that sooner or later the mist will clear and reveal the all-encompassing spectacles of peak, glacier, and forest under a sparkling sun.

The park, as established in 1968 after thirty years of agitation, is portioned into four units: two wilderness areas and two recreational areas (see map on page 26).

CLIMBERS PERCH ON THE TIP *of Magic Mountain (7,600 ft.) on the western boundary of the park's South Unit. The tough, stable rock offers a good climbing surface, and many of the precipitous peaks have been ascended by rock-climbing teams.*

NORTH CASCADES NATIONAL PARK

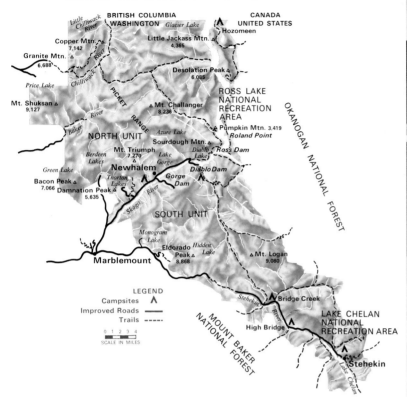

A TOPOGRAPHIC JUMBLE, *the park is apportioned into four units: two wilderness areas—North and South— and two recreational areas—Ross Lake and Lake Chelan—all administered by the National Park Service. No roads traverse the wildlands, which are laced with 345 miles of hiking and riding trails and stretches of abandoned mining and logging road. Principal access from the west: Highway 20; from the east, excursion steamer up Lake Chelan.*

WILDERNESS HEART OF *the South Unit, the Eldorado Highlands are cloaked in a massive, living glacier. The rugged mountain range is composed of deformed rock (gneiss) that is resistant to the softening forces of erosion, hence the jagged profile.*

BOB AND IRA SPRING

SMALL ICEBERGS FLOAT on the frigid waters of Trapper Lake, fed by glaciers on the slopes of Magic Mountain. Uncounted and un-named lakes abound in this wild land, much of it still unmapped. The alpine lakes are fine for fishing, some for boating, but none for swimming—far too cold.

PRINCIPAL BEACON OF THE PARK, Mount Shuksan, reflected in Priest Lake, rises above its glaciers to an elevation of 9,127 feet. Unlike other major peaks in the Cascades, Shuksan is non-volcanic in origin. A trail leads to its ice-crowned summit.

OLYMPIC

THREE GREAT PARKS IN ONE

PARK FACTS: *Location:* Olympic Peninsula, northwestern Washington. *Discovered:* 1774. *Established:* June 29, 1938. *Size:* 1,400 sq. mi. *Altitude:* Sea level to 7,965 feet. *Climate:* Summers cool and sunny, but rain likely; winters wettest in the conterminous United States. *Season:* All year, but some main roads closed by snow. *Visitors,* 1968: 2,013,800.

OF ALL THE NATIONAL PARKS, THE MOST DIVERSIFIED in character and climate is Olympic. Here you will find seacoast and mountain peak, rain forest and glacier, and an unbelievably abrupt change of weather patterns. The western side of the park has the wettest winter climate in the United States, with nearly *12 feet* of precipitation annually. The eastern side is the driest part of the Pacific Coast outside of Southern California.

Located on the Olympic Peninsula in the extreme northwest corner of Washington, the park contains one of the last virgin wilderness areas between Mexico and Canada. Through it wind hundreds of miles of hiking and horseback trails. Along the trails, as welcome retreats in case of sudden storm or the arrival of darkness, are many simple overnight shelters.

The Olympic Mountains are centered on the peninsula between the Pacific Ocean to the west and Hood Canal to the east. The land rises gently from the water and suddenly steepens, culminating in the heights of Mount Olympus. In comparison with the altitudes of inland mountains, the summit of Olympus—7,965 feet—and those of other peaks above 7,000 feet do not sound impressive. But this range rises from sea level, and it is massive. Jagged peaks shade the deep canyons, about 60 glaciers lie in the cirques, and shaggy forests climb from the sea up to timberline.

The rain forests are the strangest portions of the park, and to many the most fascinating. Their vegetation is as luxuriant as that of the Amazon jungles. Great ferns spring from beds of thick moss. Thickets of vine maple lend mystery, and gigantic trees trail heavy draperies of moss that filter the sunlight to an eerie yellow-green. There are three such forests—in the valleys of the rivers

THE SIGHT AND SOUND OF RUNNING WATER *is everywhere in this forested land. Fed by glaciers, streams run all year, reach a crescendo in summer when sun speeds melting of the ice. Rustic bridge across Soleduck Falls, in northern part of park, connects trails on each side of river.*

MARTIN LITTON

31

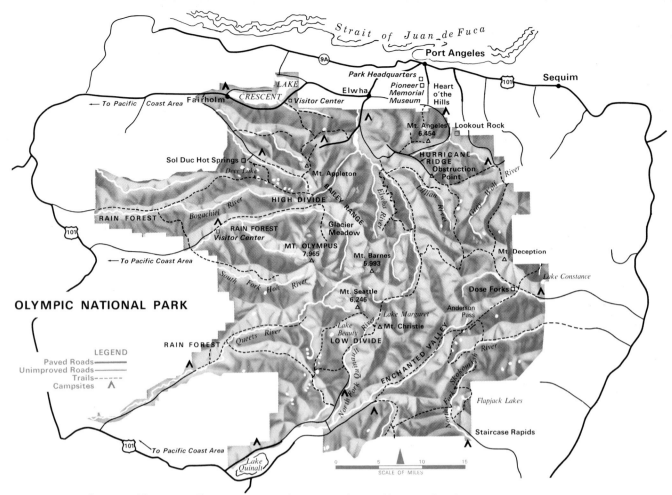

Olympic National Park is divided *into two parts: a thin coastal strip (map on page 40) and an inland block. Roads connect the two sections, but the park boundaries do not surround both. Most of the main body of the park is up-and-down country, a confusing mass of mountains and canyons.*

Fishermen troll *for rainbow and cutthroat trout on Lake Crescent, largest body of water in park, which fills a deep east-west glacial trough close to the northern boundary. Easily accessible, lake is a popular resort center.*

Hoh, Queets, and Quinault—and in them are found several of the world's largest specimens of luxuriant plant life.

About five thousand Olympic elk dwell in the park. Blacktail deer live here, and so do black bears and a host of smaller animals.

Like a few other national parks, Olympic is a land of water, and it boasts not only lakes and rivers but the ocean as well. To preserve the rugged beauty of unmodified coastline with jagged cliffs, islands, and coves, the park takes in 50 miles of shoreline, perhaps the most primitive remaining in this country.

Along with hiking, mountain climbing attracts many to Olympic. Many of the lesser peaks can be conquered in safety by the inexperienced, but the more difficult demand skill. Once attained, the heights offer views that are all-embracing —peaks on every side, snow and ice, flower-strewn meadows, and the heavy coniferous forest. Beyond are the waters of the Pacific, Strait of Juan de Fuca, and Puget Sound, and the cities and towns of northwest Washington.

No trip to this peninsula would be complete without a visit to the Indian fishing village of La Push, at the mouth of Quillayute River on the ocean strip. Here fishermen still use dugout canoes and dip nets to take silversmelt in spring.

OLYMPIC HAS HAD A LONG AND EMBATTLED HISTORY. Over a span of 40 argumentative years, it has been set up in turn as a forest preserve (1897-1909), a national monument (1909-33), and, finally, a national park (1938). It has been shifted back and forth between the Department of Interior (1897-1905, 1933 to date) and the Department of Agriculture (1905-1933), and it has ranged in size from an initial 615,000 acres, down to a low in 1915 of 300,000 acres, and back up to its present size, 896,000 acres. Its boundaries have been adjusted a half dozen times.

Principal reason for this checkered history has been strong local opposition to the park built on the conviction that it would withdraw thousands of acres of harvestable timber needed to sustain the state's giant lumbering industry. First moves to set aside the area were introduced in the 1890's, and though repeated attempts were made in later years, including a bill in 1905 to establish it as Elk National Park, the park was not created until 1938. The protracted battling surged in and out of congressional committee hearings, reached into the President's Cabinet, and even drew President Franklin Roosevelt to Port Angeles in an attempt to compromise the disputed issues. In time, proponents of the park were able to win their point that creation of the national park would bring long-run benefits to the state, as well as the nation, that would greatly outweigh the short-run benefits to be derived from logging off the trees, and the park was finally legislated into existence.

The name chosen for the park harks back to an English sea captain, John Mears, who sighted the high mountains from the coast in 1788 and named the highest peak Mount Olympus, believing it deserved the dignity of association with the Greek home of the gods. For 24 years, Olympic was known as Mount Olympus National Monument, and the park was very nearly named Mount Olympus National Park when it was established.

Rain Forest

THE LUMINOUS WORLD OF THE RAIN FOREST is filled with a soft green light reflected and refracted by the mosses and the translucent maple leaves. To a well-traveled Westerner, there are no strange or unknown organisms. Everything that grows in the rain forest, except the Sitka spruce, grows in other places. The differences are not so much in species as in habit. Water-loving things, be they microbes, mushrooms, or Douglas firs, are literally in their element. Their growth and functioning in the life community are stepped up here.

With all its exuberance, the whole forest is unexpectedly fragile. The trees are shallow-rooted, as they can be where food and water are plentiful and where the forest cover is so continuous that the wind cannot easily get a "bite."

Within the rain forest, trees grow large and undergrowth is abundant. Olympic has the world's record specimens of Douglas-fir, Western red cedar, and Western hemlock. The undergrowth, though luxuriant, is seldom impenetrable. In places it is yielding and pleasant to the touch, with winding aisles that invite strolling. The foliage is kept in check partly by the browsing of the park's most famous wild creature, the Roosevelt elk, who spend 9 months of the year here before migrating to high ground for the summer.

RUTH KIRK

ROOSEVELT ELK ROAM THE RAIN FOREST *in winter, move to the high country in summer. Also known as Olympic elk, these animals were one of the principal reasons for creation of the park, which was nearly named in their honor.*

CATHEDRAL-LIKE FORESTS *of immense Douglas fir trees with Western hemlock and Western red cedar fill river valleys.*

MARTIN LITTON

CAUSES OF WASHINGTON RAIN FOREST

1. HEAVY RAINFALL. *Caused by steep rise of mountains forcing storm clouds to ascend and release moisture.*

2. CONCENTRATED MOISTURE. *Rain plus runoff from mountain sides plus slow river flow concentrates moisture in the valley.*

3. SEA-LEVEL TEMPERATURES. *Long, almost level floor of valley extends moderate, sea-level temperatures deep inland.*

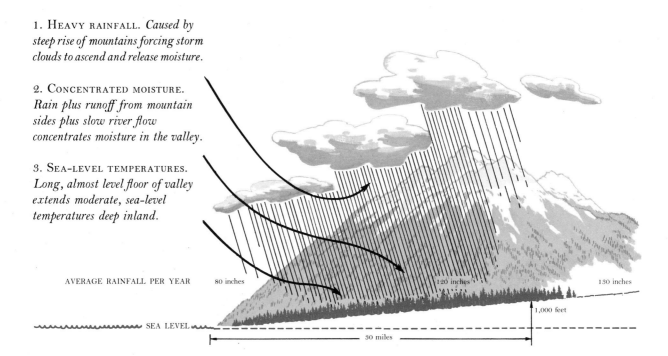

AVERAGE RAINFALL PER YEAR   80 inches   120 inches   130 inches

1,000 feet

SEA LEVEL

30 miles

MARTIN LITTON

ROADS PENETRATE *just the fringes of the park, and the only way to enjoy most of its primitive grandeur is to hike or ride horseback. A network of trails follows the stream courses through the forests. Simple trailside shelters, spaced a few miles apart, offer protection from drizzle and overnight accommodations on a first-come first-served basis.*

FILLED WITH SOFT GREEN LIGHT, *the Olympic rain forest invites the visitor to stroll down its moss-festooned paths between luxuriant growths of maidenhair, swordfern, and deer and licorice ferns.*

DAVID MUENCH

36   OLYMPIC

LIFE CYCLE OF A RAIN FOREST: *After a tree topples, forest starts to return it to soil; bacteria and fungi slowly break down its fibres; mosses cover it, give surface in which tree seeds germinate, sprout; seedling takes root; in time, a new tree grows.* RIGHT: *Key to typical plant community (*ABOVE*).*

KEY TO PLANTS IN TYPICAL
RAIN FOREST COMMUNITY

1. SITKA SPRUCE *identifies the rain forest. Its life begins on rotting logs and stumps.*

2. VINE MAPLE (Acer circinatum) *gives the deep forest a cheerful luminescence.*

3. RUNNING PINE (Lycopodium clavatum). *Common clubmoss found on trees, logs, stumps, rail fences, and the ground.*

4. FIR CLUBMOSS (Lycopodium selago).

5. SELAGINELLA (S. oregana) *forms the graceful curtains on the maple boughs.*

6. MOSS (Eurhynchium oreganum) *is one of the true mosses of the Olympic forests.*

7 AND 8. MOSSES (Rhytidiadelphus loreus *and* Rhytidiadelphus triquetrus) *typical of the rain forest, range across the continent to Evangeline's "forest primeval."*

9. BEADRUBY (Maianthemum dilatatum). *Glossy leaves highlight carpets of moss.*

10. WOOD SORREL (Oxalis oregana). *The commonest leafy plant of the forest floor.*

11. DEER FERN (Lomaria spicant). *Look for erect, thin fertile leaves in center.*

12. WESTERN SWORDFERN (Polystichum munitum). *Each leaflet has own stalk.*

13. LICORICE FERN (Polypodium vulgare) *grows on logs, stumps, rocks, mossy trees.*

14. LADY FERN (Athyrium filix-fœmina) *looks something like bracken minus stalk.*

15. FRAGRANT BEDSTRAW (Galium triflorum).

16. LICHEN (Lobaria oregana) *is colony of interdependent fungi and algae.*

Pacific Coast Area

WITH THE HARD, WET SAND UNDER FOOT, the beachhiker finds the Pacific Coast Area a fascinating realm of spray and mist, where every twisting mile reveals subtle changes in the scenery and surprises along the trail.

The wide trail picks its way through barricades of driftwood, tossed on the beach by the waves in massive piles of jackstraws. Wedged among the rocks or bobbing in the surf are occasional glass floats, broken loose from fishing nets off Japan and carried across the Pacific by the current on a year-long voyage. Here and there are battered timbers and twisted ironwork, mementos of the countless ships that have been smashed to bits against the cliffs.

In season, the running of the smelt brings out fishermen en masse; and during the clamming months, throngs of diggers, equipped with shovels and buckets, probe feverishly for razor clams that retreat deep into the sand to elude the clutching hand. An abundance of marine life thrives in the tide-pools, where it may be viewed under the guidance of ranger naturalists, who conduct walks through this chill and slippery realm.

RUTH KIRK

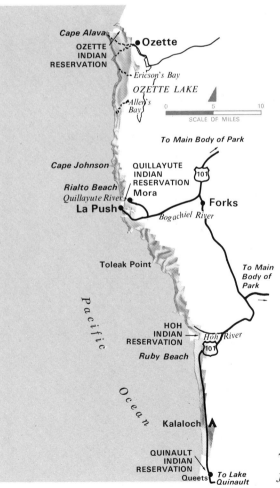

MUSSELS CROWD TOGETHER *in an intertidal environment that is so favorable that the creatures living in it multiply and compete for food and living space.*

THE COASTAL STRIP *of Olympic National Park is separated from the main body of the park that lies a few miles inland.*

Campers ignore a lowering sky *as they pitch camp on a natural jetty near Point Toleak. Damp weather does not deter those who are drawn to this dramatic coastline, a place of primeval and unspoiled grandeur.*

INQUISITIVE HARBOR SEALS *are often
seen from the beach. Squashy pawprints in
the wet sand reveal the presence of black
bear, who emerge at dusk to fish in the
surf or feed on carrion. Other permanent
residents of the strip include elk and deer,
who frequently come down to the beach,
and raccoons that catch crabs in tidepools.*

THERE IS NO WAY TO GO ASTRAY *on nature's wide trail between sea and wooded hills. Much of the 50-mile strip of sand is sandy beach, alternating with dense forests that press to the waterline. Hikers carry tide tables so they can pass headlands at low tide.*

A LONE DUGOUT CANOE, *propelled by an outboard motor, drones into the estuary of Goodman Creek bay. Indians living along the strip still use these venerable craft for offshore transportation and for fishing. Carved from a single cedar log, dugouts have been known to last 50 years or more.*

DUGOUTS AND DINGHIES *share berthing space at the dock at La Push, only seaport in the strip and center of Quillayute Indian Reservation. Boats used by Indians for deep-sea fishing for salmon. The few cedar dugouts being made today are rough-shaped with chainsaws, finished by hand.*

COMMON MURRE, *bobbing in a tidepool is one of several species of birds that nest in the nearby wildlife refuges.*

Hikers' Highlands

THE HEART OF THE PARK IS A DEDICATED MOUNTAIN WILDERNESS. Without question, it is not for everyone. Yet, even with all the aloofness of haughty Olympus itself, no other wilderness is more inviting, more unlocked, or more approachable.

This highland domain is all up-and-down country, its peaks and ridges separated by the valleys of rivers sliced so deep into the yielding rock that some have reached their ultimate level. Irregular and complex as they are, the Olympics contain two principal sections: a "wet" area that roughly faces the western boundary of the park and traps the bulk of the moisture-laden air from the Pacific Ocean, and a "dry" section that marks the eastern edge with a series of peaks separated by short, steep, river canyons. Mount Olympus, monarch of the wet range, is not easy to see from afar. Unlike its distant neighbor, Mount Rainier, which rises high above the countryside, Olympus is a puzzling cluster of crags that are barely clear of the ice cap and nearly lost in a jumble of peaks.

Few roads penetrate to this mountain fastness, and access is largely by trail—600 miles of it. Hikers familiar with conditions in the Sierra or Rockies find the Olympics easy going because of the lower altitudes, the fresh, cool weather, plentiful water, and soft, spongy trails.

THIS IS A HIKER'S PARK *that offers its best rewards to the strong-legged and self-sufficient. Trails cover a variety of terrain, from wet to dry, moss-covered to ice-encrusted. Only hikers skilled in snow and ice climbing, or those trained in the basic techniques, are permitted to ascend into the glacial highlands. The roped party above is crossing a glacier on Mount Olympus.*

BREATHTAKING VISTAS OPEN WITH *every bend in the trail that climbs to the summit of Mount Olympus. The up-and-down nature of the terrain produces long views of deep canyons and towering mountain ridges.*

OLYMPIC 47

HIGH ABOVE A CLOUD-FILLED CANYON, *deer graze on the meadows of "panorama country" in the northeast corner of the park. Hurricane Ridge is noted for its magnificent outlooks over the Strait of Juan de Fuca and the snowcapped peaks around Mount Olympus, as well as the view of the towering peaks to the east. Highest alpine area in the park that can easily be reached by automobile, Hurricane Ridge is approached by a high-grade road that rises from sea level to 5,200 feet in 18 miles.*

WILDFLOWERS BURST INTO BLOOM *while snow is still on the ground at Hurricane Ridge. Fields of alpine lilies cover the high meadowlands. The snow-covered Bailey Range looms on the horizon.*

DARWIN VAN CAMPEN

MOUNT RAINIER

SNOW-CAPPED BEACON TO A STATE

PARK FACTS: *Location:* West central Washington. *Discovered:* 1792 by Vancouver expedition, mountain named for British Admiral Rainier; area explored 1833. *Established:* March 2, 1899. *Size:* 378 sq. mi. *Altitude:* 1,914 to 14,410 feet. *Climate:* Mt. Rainier perennially snow and cloud capped. *Season:* All year. *Visitors, 1968:* 1,682,740.

ON A CLEAR DAY, THE SNOW-MANTLED CREST OF MOUNT RAINIER dominates the skyline of northwest Washington, even in cities and towns on Puget Sound more than 50 miles away. At a distance its great height and some trick of the atmosphere make it seem much closer. Those who live within sight of its gleaming peak seem to draw a sense of security and well-being from its presence; they are cheered when the clouds roll away and they can tell one another, "You can see the mountain today."

It is easy to imagine the impact the mountain had on Captain George Vancouver of the British Navy, when he cruised the Pacific Coast in 1792. He was probably the first white man to see it, and he promptly gave it its present name, in honor of his friend Admiral Peter Rainier. Later it became an unmistakable landmark for pioneers bound for the Oregon Country, who knew when they saw it that they were nearing the end of their journey.

The mountain was born of fire. It is one of several great volcanoes of the Cascade Range, and it inspired John Muir to write: "Of all the fire mountains which, like beacons, once blazed along the Pacific Coast, Mount Rainier is the noblest."

Despite the steam caves and warm mineral springs that prove the volcanic furnaces are not completely extinguished, more than one-tenth of Mount Rainier National Park's 378-square-mile area is ice. There are a dozen major glaciers, and 26 that are important enough to have names; and they are among the most accessible in the United States. Some can be reached by a short walk from the road, and several others can be viewed from close-up vantage points. Until recently, for as long as men have been studying them, the glaciers have

THIS IS MOUNT RAINIER as it reveals itself to mountain explorers based at Klapatche Lake on the western slope of Rainier. Add to this scene the tang of crisp, clean mountain air and the whisper of wind in the trees and you begin to share the secrets of "The Mountain."

BOB AND IRA SPRING

51

Up to 80 feet of snow *in one winter has been recorded in the Paradise area, a major winter recreation center. Snow lingers here well into July, and as it melts, the white fields are replaced by bright carpets of wildflowers. Located near an active glacier, Paradise offers base for glacier exploring.*

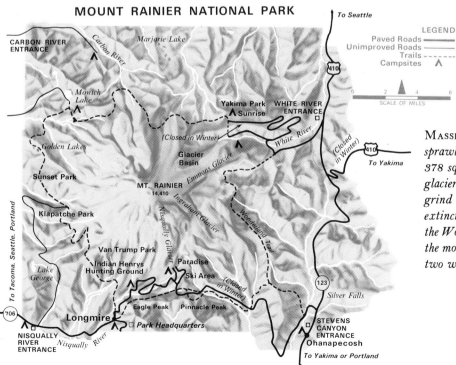

MOUNT RAINIER NATIONAL PARK

Massive Mount Rainier *sprawls over quarter of park's 378 square miles. Twenty-six glaciers covering 40 square miles grind down the slopes of the extinct volcano. Hikers' delight: the Wonderland Trail encircles the mountain in 90 miles, takes two weeks to cover.*

been gradually receding. Now they are advancing again—very slowly, of course, and perhaps only temporarily.

Below the ice fields is an unspoiled preserve of alpine meadows and dense forests, home of countless birds and animals—tiny as the chickadee, large as the black bear, rare as the mountain goat. Wildflowers brighten the lower slopes in late spring and move upward in an unfolding tapestry as the snow melts.

Rainier rations its beauty and grandeur, as if to make sure it will be appreciated. Much of the time it retires behind a heavy cloud cover; on other days it tantalizes its admirers by hiding behind a thin curtain of vapor. Then, when the mood is right, the veil suddenly is lifted, and there is the matchless crown of ice and snow shining in the sunlight.

Weather is uncertain at Mount Rainier, but a good share of warm, clear days can usually be expected between early July and mid-September, and sometimes into October, when the wooded slopes renew their annual display of autumn color. In the course of the year the park receives heavy rain and snowfall, for the Cascades are a major barrier to moisture-laden winds from the Pacific. Precipitation averages about 110 inches a year at Paradise, where as much as 80 feet of snow has fallen in a single winter to leave a snowpack of 30 feet.

Hiking is popular here, and the choice of trails ranges from short nature walks to a hike along the Wonderland Trail, which completely encircles the mountain and samples the whole variety of terrain the park has to offer. Typical of the shorter walks is the Trail of the Shadows, a special delight in spring when the rivulets are full and the air is fragrant with the odor of evergreens, damp earth, and growing things.

For those who enjoy mountain climbing, Rainier is a worthy challenge. It requires a strenuous ascent over lava, glaciers, and ice fields, though without the danger of the vertical faces to be scaled elsewhere in the West. Some 2,400 climbers—after registering in person with a ranger and obtaining weather forecasts, route condition information, and other helpful recommendations—reach the summit each year.

The park is open year round, although the Carbon River, White River, and Stevens Canyon entrances are closed from the first heavy snowfall (usually around November 1) until about the last half of June. Mount Rainier is a favorite of campers, and one of the campgrounds—Sunshine Point, near Nisqually Entrance—is available for use through the winter. On winter weekends and holidays the skiers come to Paradise.

In several ways Mount Rainier is one of the least remote of the national parks of the West. Its peak is visible over a vast area. It is one of the nearest to large centers of population. And, in a sense, it can be seen from the highway by the passerby, for the roads along the southern and eastern edges provide spectacular views of its snow-clad monarch.

But few who glimpse its beauty as they pass are satisfied until they return for a longer visit.

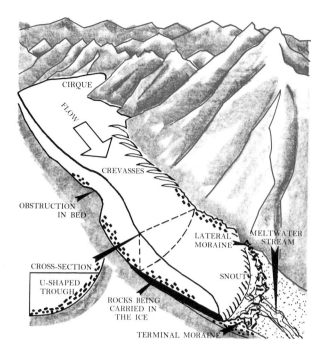

HOW DOES A GLACIER WORK?

GLACIERS ARE FORMED *where snowfall is so heavy that the winter's accumulation cannot be removed by melting in summer. The snow piles deeper and deeper, becomes denser and denser, and finally becomes solid ice. Tremendous weight of the built-up mass causes it to flow downhill at a slow pace. Where the river of ice reaches lower and warmer elevations, it melts and changes to a running stream or river, depending on its size. At the point where its progress is arrested, it forms a bulging tongue called a "snout."*

The flowing ice carries rock debris with it, some dislodged from the mountainsides, some from the bed of the valley that it occupies. This residue may give the lower end of a glacier a dirty, messy look quite unlike the pristine white of its upper reaches. In time, the rocky mass is deposited either at the sides or at the snout in massive accumulations known as moraines. The gouging processes of a glacier are most active where it starts, thus causing the formation of bowl-like cavities known as cirques.

Where glacial ice flows around sharp bends, over obstructions in its bed, or rubs against the valley wall, the brittle mass cracks open to form deep crevasses, as in the photograph (RIGHT) of the Winthrop Glacier on the north side of Mount Rainier.

BEARGRASS LINES THE SLOPES *of the Tatoosh Range. Towering in the distance: Mount Adams.*

BOB AND IRA SPRING

"A PERFECT FLOWER ELYSIUM," *is the way John Muir described the wildflower parks that encircle*
Mount Rainier. A bright wreath of ever-changing color carpets slopes between glaciers and forest.
Floral display comes in two intense seasons: first in early July, as snow recedes; second, the next month.

PAUL V. THOMAS

Canadian dogwood   *Phlox*   *Buttercup*   *Avalanche lily*

A PURPLE GLOW *infuses the ceiling and walls of ice grottos inside glaciers.
Sunlight passing through the compressed ice changes to the blue-purple side of the spectrum. Snow
climbers catch their breath in a grotto at the 10,000-foot level on Cowlitz Glacier.*

ICE-CLIMBING TOOLS

SPECIAL GEAR *is similar
to that used by rock
climbers* (see page 248).
1. ICE PITONS *and ice
screws for securing
climbing ropes.*
2. ICE AXE, *versatile
tool for cutting steps in
ice, securing rope, and
serving as a brake or
rudder for downhill
slides.*
3. CAMPONS, *steel
spikes on a frame to
be strapped to
climbing boots.*

SINCE 1833, *ascent to the 14,410-foot summit of Mount
Rainer has challenged mountain climbers. Nearly 2,400
leather-lunged climbers a year now register and make
the two-day climb to the crest.* RIGHT: *Climbers picking
their way past seracs on the Ingraham Glacier at
11,000 feet use some of same techniques as rock climbers.*

58   MOUNT RAINIER

CRATER LAKE

BLUE SAUCER ON A VOLCANO SITE

PARK FACTS: *Location:* Southwestern Oregon. *Discovered:* June 12, 1853. *Established:* May 22, 1902. *Size:* 250 sq. mi. *Altitude:* 4,405-8,926 feet. *Climate:* Snow covers park nearly 8 months of year, but main roads kept open all year. Summer weather is very unpredictable, with warm days and chilly nights. *Visitors in 1968:* 578,300.

THE KLAMATH INDIANS TELL US that long ago, before there was a Crater Lake, the volcanic mountain called Mazama served as the passageway between the domain below the earth and the world topside. When Lao, chief of the world below, visited the surface, he could be seen as a dark form towering above the white snows. When Sahale Tyee, chief of the world above, appeared on earth, he rested atop Mount Shasta, south of Mazama.

The day came when these two deities quarreled, and the anger of Lao shook the ground, sent thunder and burning ashes into the sky, and spilled lava down the mountainside.

The medicine men interpreted Lao's violence as a curse directed at least in part toward the tribe for wickedness and error. To make atonement, they climbed to the top of Mount Mazama and threw themselves into the crater.

The chief of the world above was so impressed by this sacrifice that he renewed his war with Lao and finally drove him underground. As the chief of the world below retreated and disappeared, the mountaintop fell in upon him and his door to the surface was sealed. Never again did Lao frighten the Indians; the crater of his mountain filled with pure waters and became a scene of peace and quiet.

The Indian legends have helped geologists reconstruct the violent eruptions that climaxed with the collapse of Mount Mazama's cone. The timetable is necessarily inexact, but all evidence indicates that the bowl containing Crater Lake was created within the last 10,000 years.

Before its collapse, Mazama was a 12,000-foot volcano that stood out with the mountains now called Baker, Rainier, Adams, Hood, and Shasta as giants of the Cascade Range. The peak had built up from repeated flows of molten lava

THE INTENSE BLUES of Crater Lake must be seen to be believed. Ranging from indigo to turquoise, depending on water depth, the color is thought to be caused by scattering of sunlight in water of great depth and clarity. Blue is reflected, other rays absorbed.

61

and the debris of explosive eruptions. Glaciers filled the valleys of its sculptured slopes, and thick forests covered the foothills.

The climactic eruptions recounted in legend must have been horrendous by any standards. Earthquakes were followed by enormous clouds of gases and steam that blocked out the sun for weeks. Embers and ashes fell over a vast area, covering the land with gray powder and igniting the forests. The glaciers melted and new rivers washed down the steep slopes.

And then came the greatest explosion of all. A dense cloud of dust, expanding gases, and red-hot lava fragments burst from the crater and spilled down the slopes, traveling at great speed. The avalanche crushed every form of life for 35 miles around.

Long fissures opened beneath the volcano. The violence underground continued for days, with additional eruptions and expulsions, until Mazama's peak became a heavy shell over an empty pocket. Shaken by the violence and deprived of support, the top of the volcano fell in with a roar that must literally have staggered the Indian witnesses.

When the skies finally cleared, the mountain peak was gone, and the fore-shortened slopes of Mazama rose to a huge bowl more than 5 miles across and 4,000 feet deep.

The caldera (Spanish and Portuguese for caldron) began to fill with rain and melting snow. The first pools were turned to steam by the boiling mud and hot rocks in the bottom of the basin, but as the mountain cooled the caldera filled with water. Eventually the water level reached a point higher than that of today, then receded to its present depth of about 2,000 feet.

There are many calderas in the world, but none is quite as spectacular as that of Crater Lake. The broken lines of the old volcano contrast with the quiet surface of the deep, blue water. Visitors who drive around the lake are impressed with the immensity of the mountain and the tremendous forces that caused its downfall. Geologists find Mazama one of the best places on earth to study volcanism.

Most of the park's roadways and points of interest are related to the caldera and its surrounding slopes. The major exception is the Pinnacles. These needle-like rock formations are remnants of the avalanches of volcanic pumice that preceded Mount Mazama's collapse. The pumice spread out in sheets and cooled rapidly on top, but the hot rocks beneath continued to send gases to the surface through vents. These hot emissions hardened the pumice around the vents to form "pipes." When the rest of the pumice eroded away during succeeding centuries, the pipes remained as thin pinnacles.

The Indians long believed that only punishment could come to men who looked upon a lake that was sacred to the spirits. "Do not look upon this place," the legend warned, "for it will mean death or lasting sorrow." Fortunately, the ominous warning no longer applies. The thousands who stand in awe each year on the brink of Crater Lake come away not in sorrow but with a new and exultant realization of nature's power and beauty.

HOW CRATER LAKE WAS FORMED

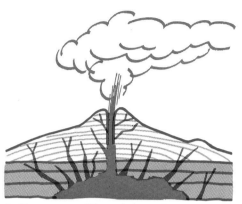

1. ERUPTIONS *of lava from crater built up Mt. Mazama over period of time.*

2. VOLCANO *spent itself in series of violent eruptions that emptied underlying lava chamber.*

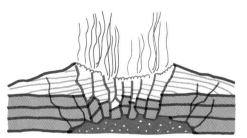

3. CAVE-IN *of top of peak, caused by withdrawal of underground support, created caldera.*

4. WATER *filled caldera to form lake. Wizard Island formed 6,000 years later by new eruption.*

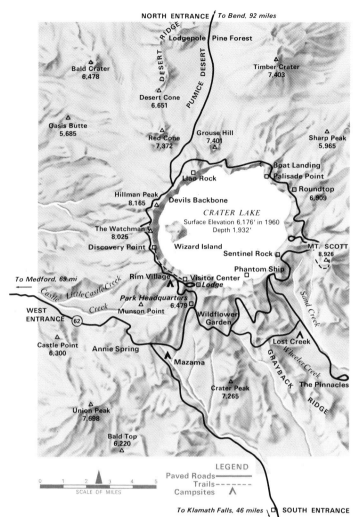

NORTH ENTRANCE / To Bend, 92 miles

Lodgepole Pine Forest
DESERT RIDGE
PUMICE DESERT

Bald Crater
6,478

Timber Crater
7,403

Desert Cone
6,651

Oasis Butte
5,685

Red Cone
7,372

Grouse Hill
7,401

Sharp Peak
5,965

Boat Landing
Llao Rock
Palisade Point
Hillman Peak
8,165
Roundtop
6,909
Devils Backbone

CRATER LAKE
Surface Elevation 6,176' in 1960
Depth 1,932'

The Watchman
8,025

Discovery Point

Wizard Island

Sentinel Rock

MT. SCOTT
8,926

To Medford, 69 mi

Castle Little Castle Creek
Creek

Rim Village
Visitor Center
Lodge

Phantom Ship

Sand Creek

Park Headquarters
6,479
Munson Point

Wildflower
Garden

WEST
ENTRANCE 62

Annie Spring

Lost Creek

Wheeler Creek

Castle Point
6,300

Mazama

GRAYBACK RIDGE

The Pinnacles

Crater Peak
7,265

Union Peak
7,698

Bald Top
6,220

LEGEND
Paved Roads
Trails
Campsites

0 1 2 3 4 5
SCALE OF MILES

To Klamath Falls, 46 miles
SOUTH ENTRANCE

CRATER LAKE NATIONAL PARK

CORE OF THE *250-square-mile national park, Crater Lake's 22 square miles of water is contained within a 20-mile circle of cliffs. Pumice flow spewed out of crater of now-dead Mount Mazama filled all valleys now within park boundaries and raced 20-30 miles to east and west. Lighter pumice, blasted into the air, was wind-borne for 80 miles, covered 5,000 square miles.*

DAVID MUENCH   WINTER CASTS *a magic spell over Crater Lake when heavy snow rims the indigo water and cloaks the firs and hemlocks with a quilt of dazzling white. Lying on the crest of the Cascade Range above 6,500 feet, the park annually receives more than 50 feet of snow, which covers much of it for nearly 8 months, starting as early as September and lasting almost to July. Access is kept open through the thick of winter, and visitors drive between towering snowbanks and enter buildings through tunnels from the cleared parking areas. The big rambling lodge (RIGHT) is shuttered and closed for the winter, but a coffee shop is kept open to thaw the sightseers and skiers.*

EVERYWHERE YOU LOOK are the black-grey-and-white Clark nutcrackers. They are crow-sized birds as common here as the jay, and just as sociable and thievish. Ravens, eagles, and falcons may sometimes be seen flying over the lake. California gulls often light on the water, and ducks and geese stop here on their migration route.

64   CRATER LAKE

THE PHANTOM SHIP, *rising dramatically above surface of the lake,
is formed of two kinds of volcanic rock: brown-black sails are of molten rock,
pale green hull of volcanic ash. Sails are part of a volcanic dike.*

HOW THE PINNACLES WERE FORMED

GLOWING AVALANCHES *once filled the
deep valleys surrounding the ancient peak
with a white-hot blanket of pumice. The
super-heated substance took years to cool,
and while it was still hot, it released
steam and gases through vents and tubes.
The hot gases cooked the walls of these
passageways into hard-baked chimneys,
and these ancient vents now stand alone
—as at the Pinnacles (RIGHT)—the
softer surrounding material having long
since been carried away by erosion.*

REDWOOD

SANCTUARY FOR THE WORLD'S TALLEST TREES

PARK FACTS: *Location:* North coast of California. *Discovered:* 1769 by Spaniards. *Established:* October 2, 1968. *Size:* 90 sq. mi. *Altitude:* Sea level. *Climate:* Damp, cool summers. *Season:* All year. *Visitors, 1968:* Uncounted.

ALONG A STRIP OF THE NORTHERN CALIFORNIA shoreline grows one of the world's most unusual trees, the coast redwood, renowned almost equally for its majestic beauty and for its commercial value as a source of lumber with many unique properties.

The towering trees, some of them a thousand years old, soar into the sky to 300 feet or more, the tallest rising higher than the torch of the Statue of Liberty. The trees grow in dense groves in a fog belt along the coast, favoring river valleys or canyons that open to the sea. In their natural state, the redwoods shed their lower branches as they mature and form a canopy a hundred feet overhead, creating the illusion of a great natural cathedral, which visitors find both inspiring and humbling. Unfortunately for the fate of the stately trees, the demand for redwood lumber is so great—it resists shrinkage, rot, and decay—that only good timber management can forestall the eventual logging of all the redwood trees in California. As a safeguard against such a disaster, thousands of acres of virgin redwoods have been set aside for perpetuity under government protection. Of this sequestered land, 28,000 acres are now, or will be, preserved within the national park system, owing to legislation passed in 1968.

Redwood National Park is a combination of state and federal parkland, pieced together in a mosaic (see map on page 72) totalling 58,000 acres, of which 30,000 is composed of existing state parks. In time, the state parks inside the boundaries of the national park will probably be donated to the federal preserve and the whole complex administered as one. Until this time, the two systems will probably operate as cooperating but separate entities.

REDWOODS FAVOR THE FOG BELT *close to the ocean, where mists roll in during the summer and as much as 100 inches of rain may fall in winter. In some groves, pink and white rhododendron blossoms brighten the mist-shrouded forest.*

PERMANENT RESIDENTS OF THE SHORELINE *section of the park, herd of 300 Roosevelt elk browses in the meadows near the sea. The protected animals are king-sized members of the deer family. Somewhat bellicose, they are best viewed from a safe distance.*

FIFTY MILES OF OCEAN FRONT *lie within the park's protective boundaries, preserved in their natural state for the enjoyment of all. At low tide, ranger naturalists conduct nature walks to the abundant tide pools. Beachcombing is forbidden here, in line with Park Service policy.*

THE STATELY TREES RISE *above a dense forest cover of ferns, rhododendrons, and other plants that thrive in the shade cast by the roof of foliage formed a hundred feet above the ground by the interweaving redwood branches.*

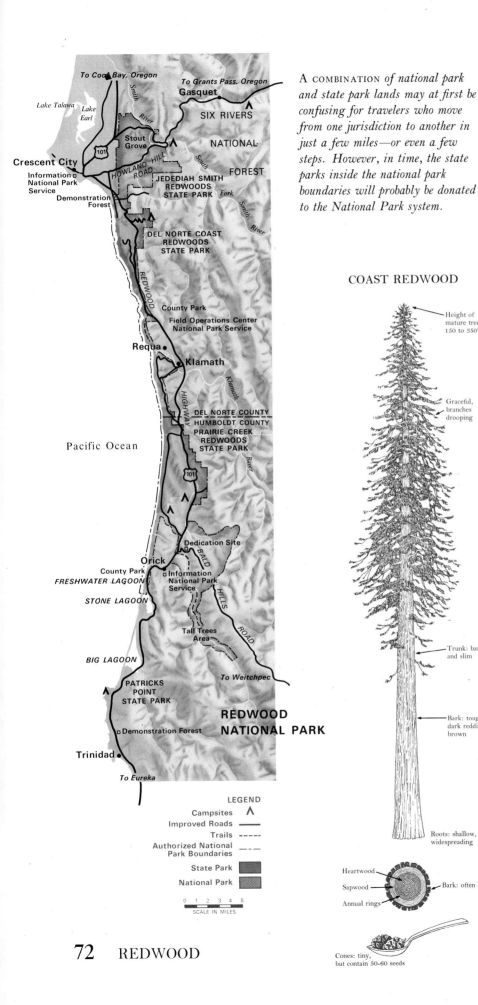

A COMBINATION of national park and state park lands may at first be confusing for travelers who move from one jurisdiction to another in just a few miles—or even a few steps. However, in time, the state parks inside the national park boundaries will probably be donated to the National Park system.

COAST REDWOOD

Height of mature trees, 150 to 350'

Graceful, branches drooping

Trunk: bare and slim

Bark: tough, dark reddish-brown

Roots: shallow, widespreading

Heartwood
Sapwood
Bark: often 1' thick
Annual rings

Cones: tiny, but contain 50-60 seeds

LEGEND

Campsites	∧
Improved Roads	——
Trails	- - - -
Authorized National Park Boundaries	— · · —
State Park	
National Park	

0 1 2 3 4 5
SCALE IN MILES

TALLEST PLANTS ON EARTH, coast redwoods are often compared with the Sierra Big Trees; redwoods were once thought to be the same species but are now known to be different. (Also see p. 117.)

ANSEL ADAMS

CENTURIES -OLD REDWOODS *owe their long life to a combination of factors. Their thick bark is virtually fireproof and the wood itself is so water-laden that it offers poor fuel for fire once it breaches the bark. In addition, the trees are saturated with tannin, a substance that resists fungi, rot, and parasites.*

REDWOOD 73

LASSEN VOLCANIC

THE SMOKE CLOUD ROSE FIVE MILES

PARK FACTS: *Location:* Northern California. *Discovered:* Probably in early 1800's. *Established:* August 9, 1916. *Size:* 160 sq. mi. *Altitude:* 4,822-10,457 feet. *Climate:* Warm, pleasant summers; snow in winter. Snow recreation area kept open in winter in southern section of the park; other areas closed. *Visitors in 1968:* 442,755.

WHEN THE FIRST WHITE SETTLERS CAME to northeastern California, they assumed that volcanic Lassen Peak was extinct. The earth around it was pockmarked with bubbling sinks, but the mountain itself appeared cold and lifeless.

But on May 30, 1914, they changed their minds. Without warning, a great column of steam and gases spouted from the top of the peak, throwing out small pieces of lava and debris on the upper slopes. The eruption was brief, but it opened a new vent in the old crater and signaled the beginning of renewed activity that lasted more than two years.

Lassen erupted more than 150 times during the next year, spouting dust and steam high in the air and flinging cinders and small boulders around its base. But no lava appeared, and spectators were more curious than concerned.

During the winter of 1914-15, snowfall was unusually heavy. It piled deep on the upper slopes of Lassen, and all that fell within the new crater immediately melted and drained down into the earth. Some scientists believe that this build-up of water below the surface was partly responsible for what happened in the spring.

On the evening of May 19, molten lava bubbled up to the crater rim. On the southwest edge, it trickled over and flowed a thousand feet down the side before cooling into a solid sheet. On the northeast side, a much more dramatic performance was developing. Lava spilled over the rim, steam roared out of a hole in the mountainside near the top, and chunks of lava fell on the slopes. The heat melted the deep drifts of snow, and this water combined with the debris of earlier eruptions to create a devastating mudflow. The deluge of mud surged down the mountain, growing in volume and violence, and funneled into the

QUIESCENT LASSEN PEAK *looms above the scene of its devastating eruptions of 1914-15. The skeletal tree is one of the few remaining of the thousands that were flattened in a few seconds by a violent blast of steam down the side of the mountain in 1915.*

valleys of Hat and Lost Creeks. It peeled the bark off trees up to 18 feet and submerged the meadows with as much as 6 feet of debris.

Despite this cataclysm, Lassen Peak was not yet spent. Three days later a spectacular column of smoke mounted 5 miles into the air and a blast of steam shot out of the mountainside. This time the force of the steam jet was horizontal. Trees in its path were knocked down like matchsticks, and the earth was scrubbed bare.

With that release of pressure, Lassen seemed all but appeased. The volcano shuddered a few more times—there were eight minor eruptions in June, six in July—but by 1921 all visible activity had subsided.

There are still many signs of these volcanic eruptions—which are the most recent in the United States except for Hawaii and Alaska—but nature is gradually covering the wounds. The devastated area is clearly defined, although a few trees are taking root in the rocky crust. You can hike to the top of Lassen Peak and look into the crater, but the crucible has long since cooled and the mountain once again wears a cap of perpetual snow.

Well below the surface, however, the volcanic pot is still boiling. At those places where the crust is broken or cracked (there are six within the park), gases and steam hiss up through fumaroles and keep the mud bubbling like porridge on a hot stove. Sulfurous vapors taint the air.

Although the 1915 eruption poured forth molten lava, Lassen is actually a plug volcano, made of stiff lumps of lava pushed upward by subterranean forces but too thick to flow like liquid. Not old, it was probably formed no more than a few thousand years ago.

There are other significant examples of volcanism in Lassen Volcanic National Park. South of Lassen Peak are traces of another giant that once existed here—Mount Tehama, a huge cone 15 miles in diameter and 11,000 feet high. It eventually collapsed, and the fractured remnants include Brokeoff Mountain, Mount Diller, Pilot Pinnacle, Mount Conard, and Diamond Point.

Chaos Crags are the remains of four plug volcanoes, much like Lassen but without craters. Prospect Peak, Mount Harkness, Red Mountain, and Raker Peak are shield volcanoes similar to those of Hawaii—volcanoes that have been built up from layers of molten lava that flowed out and then cooled into "shields."

What about the future of Lassen Peak? Will it awaken again, or has it settled into a deep and lasting sleep? Many geologists believe the volcano is well on its way to extinction. The thermal activity underground continues, but only a few wisps of steam are ever seen atop the mountain. Another series of eruptions would come as a great surprise.

Of course, that's what they were saying back in 1913.

SMOKE COLUMN *from the 1915 eruption climbed 5 miles into the sky and was visible for 50 miles; 5-ton rock bombs were catapulted into the air. Touring party watches pyrotechnic display from a discreet distance.*

LASSEN VOLCANIC NATIONAL PARK

44
89

To Redding
and Route 99 ←

44

LASSEN

PARK

Chaos
Jumbles

Manzanita Lake Lodge
Visitor Center

Manzanita
Lake

ROAD

Chaos Crags

Raker Peak
7,483

Hat Cr.

Lost

Cr.

Manzanita Cr.

Hat Mt.

Prospect Peak
8,338

Butte
Lake

Cinder
Cone

Painted
Dunes

Fantastic
Lava Beds

Cluster Lakes

Snag
Lake

Mt. Hoffman

LASSEN PEAK
10,457

Mt. Diller

Bumpass
Hell

Diamond Peak

Kings Creek
Meadows

Kings Creek
Falls

Kings

Cr.

Horseshoe
Lake

Crystal Cliffs

Juniper
Lake

Sulphur
Works

Brokeoff Mt.

Ski Area

SOUTH ENTRANCE

Mt. Conard

To Mineral

89
36

Hot Springs Cr.

Drakesbad

Boiling Springs Lake

Red Mt.

Mt. Harkness

Bonte Peak

To Chester

0   1   2   3
SCALE OF MILES

LEGEND
Paved Roads ———
Unpaved Roads ———
Trails ------
Campsites ∧

EVIDENCE OF VOLCANIC activity dots the park landscape with cones, craters, fumaroles, vents.

77

THE MOONSCAPE TERRAIN *of Chaos Jumbles was created about 300 years ago when great rockslides of pink lava chunks, possibly triggered by steam explosions along the base of the crags, rolled down the mountainside and covered about 2 square miles.*

FALL COMES EARLY *to Manzanita Lake and touches the alders and cottonwoods with orange and gold after the first snows fall. Thus ends a short but luxuriant display of wildflowers that thrive in the park. Spring reveals Indian paintbrush, bleeding heart, monkey flowers, tiger lilies, and a host of other blooms, many of which persist throughout summer. The showy red snowplant is abundant, and in the higher mountain meadows, mountainheath, lupine, and penstemon put on their finest display in mid-August. Orange wallflower, bog Kalmia, senecio, balsam root, marsh marigold, monkshood, shooting stars, the dainty white rein orchid, and blue, false forget-me-not carpet the meadows or brighten the forest trails from early June to late September.*

78   LASSEN VOLCANIC

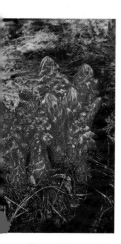

Snowplant   *Penstemon*   *Indian paintbrush*   *Leopard lily*   *Lupine*

A VOLCANO BLOWS ITS TOP

FROM REFLECTION LAKE *the eruption, only 4 airline miles away, was a spectacular sight. Over the centuries, stiff pasty lava, too cool and viscous to flow downhill, squeezed up like toothpaste from a tube to form a dome-shaped peak rising 2,500 feet above its base.*

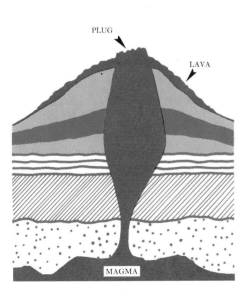

PLUG

LAVA

MAGMA

TRANQUIL MANZANITA LAKE *reflects a very different scene from the one it mirrored a half century ago. The mineral-rich soil and plentiful water encourage luxuriant growth of conifers and shrubby plants. Birds nest in the willow and alder thickets, orchids bloom in the bogs, and deer and bear seek the water at dusk.*

LASSEN VOLCANIC **81**

CINDER CONE *rises symmetrically, 700 feet above the countryside.*
A true volcano (it erupted in 1851), it was formed of lava that cooled
when it reached the air and dropped in an even fall of cinders.

BOILING MUD POTS *fling blobs of red*
mud into the air, forming a rim around
the vent. Color comes from iron oxide
in the soil. The mud is dangerously hot—
about 200° Fahrenheit.

BUMPASS HELL IS NAMED *for a pioneer who suffered the misfortune of plunging a leg into the steaming mud while showing the area to a visiting newspaperman. The rising steam and hissing vents give evidence of the thermal tumult that is close to the surface here.*

YOSEMITE

ICE, THE GREAT SCULPTOR

PARK FACTS: *Location:* East central California. *Discovered:* 1849. *Established:* State park, 1864; national park, 1890. *Size:* Approx. 1,200 sq. mi. *Altitude:* 2,000 to 13,114 feet. *Climate:* Dry, mild summers; relatively warm winters with heavy snow pack. *Season:* Valley, all year; high country, summer only. *Visitors, 1968:* 2,282,000.

"AS I LOOKED AT THE GRANDEUR OF THE SCENE a peculiar exalted sensation seemed to fill my whole being, and I found my eyes in tears with emotion." So wrote one of the discoverers of Yosemite Valley in 1851, recording an experience that has moved thousands of visitors who have since followed the trail into the Incomparable Valley.

Although it represents less than one-half of one percent of the total area of the park, the Valley contains more than its share of scenic beauty, and, historically, it accounts for the very existence of Yosemite as a national park.

The valley was known to the Indians for centuries, but because of its remoteness and inaccessibility it was not discovered by white men until the 1850's, when the Gold Rush attracted thousands of inquisitive miners to the nearby foothills and made its disclosure inevitable. It was a pair of miners, tracking a wounded bear in 1849, who were the first Americans to see the Valley. They were followed two years later by a punitive expedition, known as the Mariposa Battalion, that entered the Valley in pursuit of marauding Indians. Convinced that they had made an important discovery, they named the Valley, calling it "Yosemite" for the Indians they had driven out. The name was from an Indian word "Uzumati," meaning grizzly bear.

Word of the discovery was slow in spreading, but by 1855 the first tourist parties had followed Indian trails into the Valley to look at the reported wonders. One enterprising young miner by the name of James Hutchings was so impressed by what he saw that he launched into the business of attracting and serving tourists. He started a journal, *Hutchings California Illustrated* that featured Yosemite, published a series of guidebooks to the area, and built a hotel in the

A THREE-QUARTER MOON *rises over the shoulder of snow-dusted Half Dome, evoking the magic that enchants the visitor to Yosemite. First white man to see the great monolith named it "Rock of Ages," but the name did not stick. The rock rises 4,800 feet above the Valley floor.*

ANSEL ADAMS

85

Valley. Soon afterward, other hotels were opened, toll routes built, and the Valley began to welcome tourists of a sufficiently durable cast to survive the long and arduous trip by stage and saddle horse.

While commercial development was in progress, agitation for protection of the natural beauty of the park was also under way. John Muir and others published articles extolling the glories of the Valley, congressional interest in the area was aroused, and in 1864 President Lincoln issued the historic proclamation that ceded the Valley and the Mariposa Grove of Big Trees to California, "to be held for public use, resort, and recreation, unalienable for all time."

The Valley and the Mariposa Grove, 35 miles apart, were administered as a state park for 42 years before being returned to the federal government in 1906. In the meantime, a national park was established in 1890 that surrounded the original grant, and Yosemite was thus administered as two separate parks for 16 years. Administration of the national park was largely entrusted to units of the United States Cavalry until 1916.

Within the 1,200 square miles of the park today, there is of course a great deal more to see than the wonders compressed within the Valley. Glaciers, giant sequoias, alpine meadows, 13,000-foot Sierra peaks, emerald lakes, and sparkling streams are scattered in profusion throughout the vast domain. Those who know the park well know it as a rich and varied playground that is capable of sustaining years of rewarding exploration.

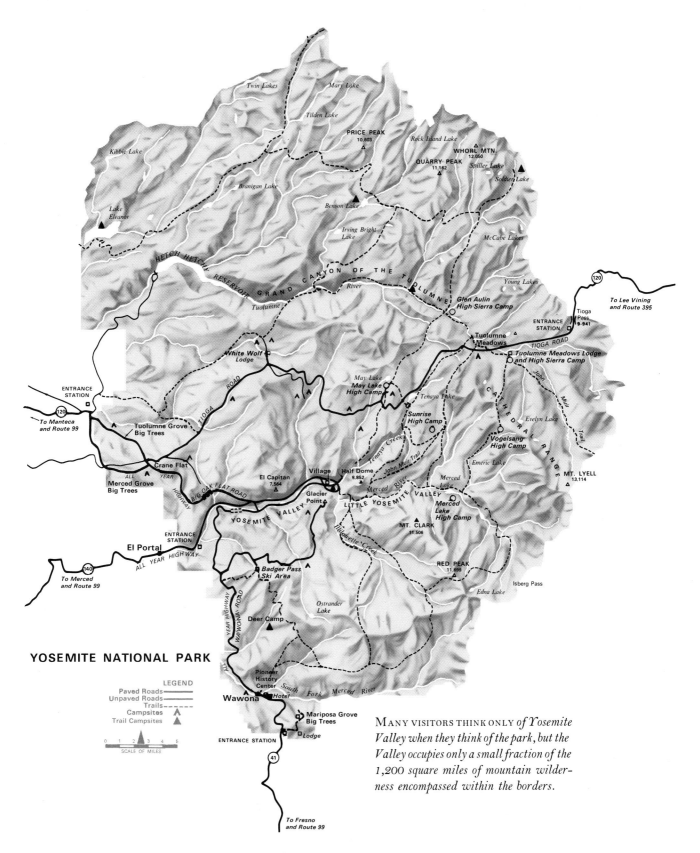

YOSEMITE NATIONAL PARK

LEGEND
Paved Roads
Unpaved Roads
Trails
Campsites
Trail Campsites

0 1 2 3 4 5
SCALE OF MILES

MANY VISITORS THINK ONLY *of Yosemite Valley when they think of the park, but the Valley occupies only a small fraction of the 1,200 square miles of mountain wilderness encompassed within the borders.*

PRESIDENT THEODORE ROOSEVELT *and a distinguished party guided by John Muir pause before passing through the Wawona Tree in the Mariposa Grove. Roosevelt's 1903 visit to the park encouraged him to press for protective legislation to save more Big Trees and other valuable natural wonders. The Wawona tree fell during a late winter storm in 1969.*

YOSEMITE **87**

The Valley

FOR WELL OVER A CENTURY, the fabled grandeur of Yosemite Valley has drawn enchanted travelers to the park. The majesty of the granite cliffs rising above the forested floor, the beauty of the tumbling waterfalls, and the tranquility of the Merced River have combined to mesmerize generations of Americans.

The Valley is a profound gorge, cut by a river and gouged by glaciers, that is 7 miles long, a mile wide, and 3,000 feet deep. Its walls are actually mountain-sized rocks, separated from each other by side canyons. So deep did the glaciers and the river cut into the granite, that they left behind the tributary streams, which cascade from hanging valleys around the rim of the canyon in waterfalls of extraordinary height.

As the central tourist attraction of the park, it is here that most of the recreational opportunities and accommodations are found. All roads into the park end at Yosemite Village. Despite the efforts of the Park Service to shunt visitors to other sections of the park, hordes of tourists pour into the compact canyon on long summer weekends. The congestion partly cancels the value of coming to the park—but it is understandable. Once seen and felt, the Valley becomes a part of the beholder, and it is with reluctance that he settles for anything less.

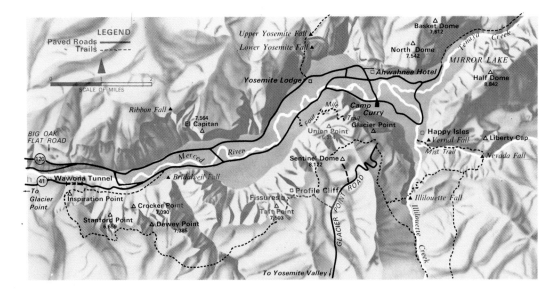

WITHIN A GLACIAL VALLEY *7 miles long and 1 mile wide are concentrated most of the spectacular domes, cliffs, and waterfalls in the park. Here, too, are the major resorts and campgrounds, located along the Merced River.*

YOSEMITE FALLS, ONE OF THE HIGHEST *in the world (2,425 ft.), tumbles over the north wall in spring with a vigor that shakes the ground, then wanes to a trickle by September.*

DAVID MUENCH

THE FALLS OF YOSEMITE *are world-renowned
for their height and beauty. Bridalveil Fall
runs a solid torrent in spring, exploding in
clouds of mist where it strikes the rocks at its
base, 620 feet below; in low-water months it
turns into a thin, gossamer veil—whence its name.*

THE FULL FORCE OF THE MERCED RIVER *pours over Vernal
Fall (317 ft.) and races down the canyon in foaming
violence. The head of the fall, a popular hike, is reached
by the Mist Trail, a slippery, spray-drenched climb. When
the sunlight is right, a rainbow forms in the mist.*

LARGER THAN THE ROCK OF GIBRALTAR, *El Capitan stands
sentinel at the lower end of the valley. Said to be the largest
single block of granite in the world, its sheer cliff attracts
rock climbers.*

DAVID MUENCH

AUTUMN FLASHES BRIGHTLY *in Yosemite Valley, helping to relieve the somber cast of the conifer forest. Within the Valley is a concentration of broadleafed trees that brings forth a more varied display of fall color than in the Yosemite forest in general. At higher altitudes, off the Tioga Road and the highway to Glacier Point, are groves of aspen that turn to shimmering gold in autumn.*

RIPPLELESS MIRROR LAKE *reflects without flaw the rugged profile of Mount Watkins, named for a pioneer photographer whose stereoscopic views of Yosemite (1861) helped to introduce its grandeurs to the nation. A changeable lake, it freezes in winter and dries up in late summer after the end of the run-off. Easter sunrise services are held in this serene setting.*

HOW YOSEMITE VALLEY WAS FORMED

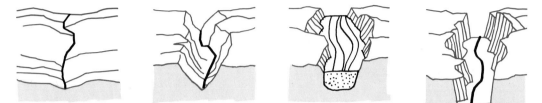

1. BROAD VALLEY STAGE   2. V-SHAPED CANYON STAGE   3. GLACIAL STAGE   4. POST-GLACIAL STAGE

GLACIERS FORMED YOSEMITE VALLEY *during the Ice Age. 1. First, the land now occupied by the Sierra was covered with low ridges, rolling hills, and broad valleys. The ancestral Merced River flowed gently. 2. A gradual upheaval tilted the Sierra block, causing the sluggish Merced to rush seaward, carving a 2,000-foot, V-shaped canyon. 3. A change in climate caused ice to accumulate in the high country. In time, glaciers gouged the valley to U-shape and rounded the peaks to domes. 4. The glaciers advanced and receded three times, then melted and left a lake dammed behind the terminal moraine. Eventually, the lake dried up, leaving the level floor of today's meadows.*

CAMP CURRY'S FIRE FALL.

"LET THE FIRE FALL!" *bellowed a stentorian voice at Curry Village in the Valley, and in a moment the first response drifted down from the summit 3,200 feet overhead: "The fire falls!" Then down into the night a cascade of embers fell halfway down the cliff. This famous spectacle enthralled visitors from 1872 to 1969 when it was discontinued at the request of the Park Service. The firey show was a favorite subject for postcard writers, as the 1920 sample on the left indicates.*

"DEER AND BEAR ARE WILD AND DANGEROUS *animals!" warns the park brochure and every bulletin board within the boundaries. Yet some tourists find them fascinating and get as close to them as they dare—sometimes to the animal's annoyance, as when photographers surround a puzzled deer; and sometimes to the animal's delight, as when a bear discovers camper's food cached in an open car.*

CAMPING DELUXE IN CONCRETE-SLAB TENT-HOUSES *along the Merced River is one of the several ways that the traveler finds shelter within the park, where accommodations range from luxury hotel to open campgrounds redolent with cedar smoke from the punky campfires. Though crowded during the summer, the camps and resorts offer an idyllic grace period just before and after the season, when the park is uncrowded and the visitor can enjoy the spectacular surroundings in relative peace and quiet.*

96 YOSEMITE

"THE GRAND WINTER STORMS," *wrote John Muir, "seldom set in before the end of November. The fertile clouds, descending, glide about and hover in brooding silence, as if thoughtfully examining the forests and streams with reference to the work before them; then small flakes or single crystals appear, glinting and swirling in zigzags and spirals; and soon the thronging feathery masses fill the sky and make darkness like night."*

North Country

NORTH OF YOSEMITE VALLEY, a 700-square-mile province of forest, rivers, and mountains spreads to the boundaries of the park. This is a land of solitude, of fresh and unspoiled country, inviting and accessible alike to hiker, camper, and motorist. Traversed by a single east-west highway, which crosses the highest pass (9,941 ft.) of any road in the state, the area is spotted with campgrounds and laced with trails that radiate from beautiful Tuolumne Meadows.

It was from the north that the first tourist routes penetrated to the Valley after it became known to the public in the 1850's. The first travelers entered the Valley on horseback, spending 12 saddle-sore hours on the rough trail. For 22 years the only access was by foot or on a horse, then toll wagon roads were opened in 1874 and 1883. Most notorious of these was the famous Tioga Road, a hair-raising mining road that was not completely modernized for 78 years. The old roads form the basis of the present intensively-used highways.

NATIONAL PARK SERVICE

STAGE PASSENGERS RODE ENVELOPED *in a cloud of dust on the Big Oak Flat Road, one of two toll roads that entered the Valley from the northwest in 1874. The narrow road zigzagged down the north wall of the canyon by a series of switchbacks. Passengers endured 20 hours of jouncing in the ride from the railhead. The toll road operated for 35 years and was put out of business when a railroad reached El Portal near the park's west boundary.*

THE LAKE BACKED UP BEHIND HETCH HETCHY DAM *fills a beautiful glacial canyon similar to Yosemite Valley. It was created after a bitter 10-year battle between conservationists and the city of San Francisco. Wrote John Muir, "Dam Hetch Hetchy! As well dam for water-tanks the people's cathedrals and churches, for no holier temple has been consecrated by the heart of man." The contest begun in 1903 was ended by congressional approval of the dam in 1913 and its construction in 1923. It is accessible by automobile from the Big Oak Flat Road.*

SKIMMING ALONG THE EDGE *of the north rim of Yosemite Valley, the Tioga Road reveals to the motorist the shining land of the High Sierra that once belonged only to the hiker and backpacker. Great vistas sweep into view at frequent intervals. Here is a look down Tenaya Canyon, with the familiar cap of Half Dome at the right, Cloud's Rest at the left.*

ORIGINALLY BUILT IN *1883 as a wagon road to service a mine, the Tioga Road was completely modernized for 78 years, and driving it was a nerve-racking adventure. Until its realignment in 1961, many miles were still in the same condition as the vintage scene at the left.*

THE NORTH COUNTRY SEEN FROM THE AIR *takes on dramatic qualities when coated with early snow. In November, when this photograph was taken, the first storms are often relatively light. The highway is covered and Tenaya Lake gleams like a bright emerald set in the cottony landscape. Within a few weeks, the snow will pile deeper, the lake will freeze to a sheet of paraffin, and the road will be lost to sight until the end of May.*

100 YOSEMITE

GATEWAY TO THE NORTH COUNTRY, *Tuolumne Meadows (8,700 ft.) is regarded as one of the most beautiful subalpine meadows in the Sierra. Sparkling air, a feeling of spaciousness, and the quiet absence of crowds endears the area to its devotees. Trails to High Sierra destinations fan out from the meadow, which is itself one stop in a loop of five High Camps, one of the most popular week-long hikes in the park.*

THE HAUNTING SONG OF MULE BELLS *sounds clearly in the still mountain air as a pack train leaves for a fishing rendezvous in the high country.*

WATCHDOGS OF THE HIGH TRAILS, *marmots are often seen above timberline. Their shrill whistles inform their relatives up the trail that nonmarmots are approaching. These self-important little animals are cousins of the prairie dog, but found only at higher elevations.*

YOSEMITE 103

South of the Valley

In the richly diversified area south of the Valley, most of the main attractions are located right on the highway.

Climbing out of the Valley, the road pauses at a turnout for a last sweeping view of the canyon, then winds upward through conifer forests. It passes Badger Pass, a crowded ski center in winter and a quiet wildflower park in summer, and ends at the tip of Glacier Point, a breathtaking overlook. Here, pressed against the guard rails, the traveler can look down 3,200 feet to the floor of the Valley or up the great gorges whence came the glaciers that carved it.

Continuing south, the highway passes through bucolic Wawona, one of the earliest settlements in the park and location of a hotel that has been serving the touring public since 1875. Nearby is the park's prime historical exhibit: a frontier village recreated from pioneer buildings gathered from all over the park. Finally, the road sidetracks to the cathedral-like groves of Big Trees, containing some of the finest and largest specimens in the state.

Nearly buried under a mat of snow, *Badger Pass Ski House is the center of a carefully planned ski area that accommodates up to 4,000 skiers on a weekend without detracting from the scenic values of the park.*

SKIERS TURN OUT EN MASSE *at Badger Pass to enjoy the runs down the tree-mantled slopes. In operation since the 1930's, Badger is popular with skiers in the Central Valley who are only an hour or two away from the resort and can drive up for a few hours or a weekend of sport.*

FRESH, UNSCORED SNOW *records the exuberance of a party of skiers on their way to the point.*

FORREST JACKSON

106 YOSEMITE

FROM GLACIER POINT, *a breathtaking sweep of Yosemite high country, diffused with what John
Muir called "good-night alpenglow," spreads to the horizon under a mountain sunset. Two great glacial
canyons sweep around Half Dome and enter the Valley: to the left, Tenaya Canyon; to the right,
the Little Yosemite, through which the Merced River flows, down Nevada and Vernal falls.*

DAVID MUENCH

"ONE OF THE MOST PHOTOGRAPHED *trees in the world,*" *is the tenacious
Jeffrey pine on the top of Sentinel Dome, a mile from Glacier Point.
The lightning-scarred and stunted tree draws its sustenance from cracks in
the granite. In a forest, the Jeffrey is often mistaken for yellow pine
and normally grows straight and tall, ranging from 60 to 170 feet.*

YOSEMITE CREEK DROPS *down from a hanging valley to join the Merced River, which in geologic ages past once ran on the same level. Best view of the full sweep of Yosemite Falls is from Sentinel Dome or Glacier Point. The Upper Fall drops 1,430 feet, probably the longest fall of its kind in the world.*

STOPPING PLACE FOR PRESIDENTS *and a favorite of vacationing families since the 1880's, peaceful Wawona in the south end of the park exudes an old-fashioned tranquility. Though fully modernized, the gingerbread buildings look the same today as they did when this photograph was taken in the 1930's or when they were built (left to right, 1889 and 1917).*

A FIELDSTONE JAIL, LOG CABINS, *and early clapboard buildings from all over the park were carefully taken apart, transported, and reassembled at the Pioneer History Center at Wawona. Nearby stands the only covered bridge in a national park. It served the park's first highway from 1857 to 1931.*

GNARLED GRIZZLY GIANT, *fifth largest of the Sierra Big Trees, is probably the fastest growing tree in the Mariposa Grove. Latest estimates place its age at 2,700 years and it still grows faster than trees half its age.*

SEQUOIA AND KINGS CANYON

BIGGEST TREES, DEEPEST CANYONS

PARK FACTS: *Location:* Southeastern California. *Discovered:* Sequoia, 1853. *Established:* Sequoia, Sept. 25, 1890; Kings, March 4, 1940. *Size:* Sequoia, 604 sq. mi.; Kings, 710 sq. mi. *Altitude:* Sequoia, 1,700-14,491 ft.; Kings, 4,600-14,242 ft. *Climate:* Summers hot; winters snowy. *Visitors, 1968:* Sequoia, 868,650; Kings, 1,060,870.

THE TWIN PARKS, SEQUOIA AND KINGS CANYON, located next to each other on the ridgepole of California, are administered as one and share many features in common.

Within the boundaries of each are several thousand acres of sequoias, the largest trees on earth. Each park encompasses a hikers' domain of spectacular peaks and canyons, threaded with an intricate trail system. The two parks are accessible to the same highway on the west, and they share the opposite ends of one of the most spectacular roads in the park system, the Generals Highway, that runs along the shoulder of a mountain ridge and reveals sweeping views of high mountains and deep valleys.

SEQUOIA, THE SECOND OLDEST NATIONAL PARK, was established in 1890 as a sanctuary of 252 square miles to protect the largest remaining sequoia groves from the logging destruction that had befallen their larger and more accessible neighbors.

The trees were considered a species of the genus (also containing *Sequoia sempervirens*, the coast redwood) which had been named for Sequoyah, inventor of the Cherokee alphabet. The giant sequoia (common name), Big Tree (poetic and unmistakable), Wellingtonia (British), Sierra redwood (Forest Service) are one and the same: *Sequoia gigantea*, which most authorities are now giving a new, unmusical name, *Sequoiadendron giganteum*.

The largest tree (by volume) in the world, the sequoia is a relic of a pre-glacial genus that was once distributed over much of the world. During the Ice Age, glaciers swept away all but the few stands in the Sierra that had been

"SEE ONE BIG TREE and you want to see another and then another," so say the visitors to the Big Tree groves. To many, it is not the size or the age of the sequoias that is the most appealing, but their mystic beauty. Few other trees possess such powers of enchantment.

DAVID MUENCH

Sequoia National Park is named for the great redwood trees which in turn were named for a Cherokee Indian, Sequoyah (ca. 1760-1843), who invented an alphabet of 86 characters for his tribe and taught his fellows to read and write. His deeds so impressed the Austrian botanist who named the redwoods that he registered the trees under the name sequoia. In Cherokee language, the name had an odd meaning: as nearly as it can be translated it meant "neither this nor that" and it was appropriately applied to the opossum.

growing on land higher than the obliterating ice. These residues of a once-encompassing forest now constitute the groves that are mostly within the protection of the two national parks and adjoining national forests.

Extensive as the present-day groves appear to be, nothing that can be seen today begins to match the vast sequoia forest that was still intact just a century ago. Between 1862 and 1900, logging operations wiped out the finest forest in the world, containing at least two trees—and possibly four or more—that must have been bigger than the world's largest tree, the General Sherman in Sequoia's Giant Grove. Ironically, two of these giants were not cut for their wood, but simply so that sections of their trunks could be exhibited at two world's fairs.

At an early date, public-spirited citizens and conservationists became alarmed by the rapidity with which lumbering activities were destroying the Big Trees. One of the last straws was the building of a sawmill about 9 miles from the Giant Forest, as part of an ill-fated co-operative colony. Determined action resulted in creation of the national park that placed the trees under permanent protection. President Harrison signed the bill creating Sequoia National Park on September 25, 1890. Established at 252 square miles, the park was enlarged 36 years later to its present 604.

For 24 years after the park was established, it was administered by the Army. Congress did not appropriate sufficient funds to support a resident administration, and the development of facilities and trails was entrusted to cavalry units that served in the park during the summer months. The troops withdrew each fall and left the area open for 9 months of poaching, trespassing, and illegal grazing. In time, adequate sums were appropriated, and the park administration was taken over by civilian administrators in 1914. Under the direction of a sequence of able and dedicated superintendents and enlightened concessioners, the park has been developed with integrity and naturalness.

The distinction of being both one of the oldest and one of the newer national parks belongs to Kings Canyon. When the park was established in 1940, it absorbed tiny General Grant National Park—the 50-year-old sanctuary that had been established almost as an afterthought a week after Sequoia was created in 1890—and has been administered by Sequoia ever since. It is now known as the General Grant Grove.

The Kings Canyon area had been proposed for park status long before the move was approved by Congress. John Muir campaigned for it in 1891 and the idea was reopened in 1926 at the time Sequoia was more than doubled in size.

The park bears the name of the river, named by a Spanish explorer in 1805 for the Three Wise Men—*El Rio de los Santos Reyes*, The River of the Holy Kings.

AN ENTERPRISING FORM OF THE VANDALISM *that ravaged the sequoia groves in the late 1800's was this project that involved stripping bark from a tree and reassembling it at the Chicago Worlds Fair in 1893, where many fairgoers thought it a fake. Its stump is now known as the Chicago Stump.*

SEQUOIA AND KINGS CANYON   115

The Big Trees

WITHIN THE REDWOOD GROVES of Sequoia and Kings Canyon National Parks stand several thousand giant sequoias, the largest trees in the world.

Hundreds of these giants far outstrip the largest specimens of any other species. Many sequoia stumps show more than 3,000 annual growth rings, and it is a safe guess that some of the trees now standing were alive in the Bronze Age, 3,500 to 4,000 years ago. Largest of them all is Sequoia's General Sherman, conceded to be the biggest of the world's measured trees. Second place is usually assigned to the General Grant Tree in Kings Canyon, and third and fourth rank respectively to the Frank E. Boole and Hart trees.

The great trees owe their long lifespan partly to a natural vigor that makes them outgrow all other species in a forest complex and partly to their thick, disease and fire-resistant bark that permits them to survive forest fires and the ravages of insect blight. Although the sequoias in the parks are among the last of their species, they are reproducing themselves adequately to continue in existence until the next Ice Age—providing Man leaves them in peace.

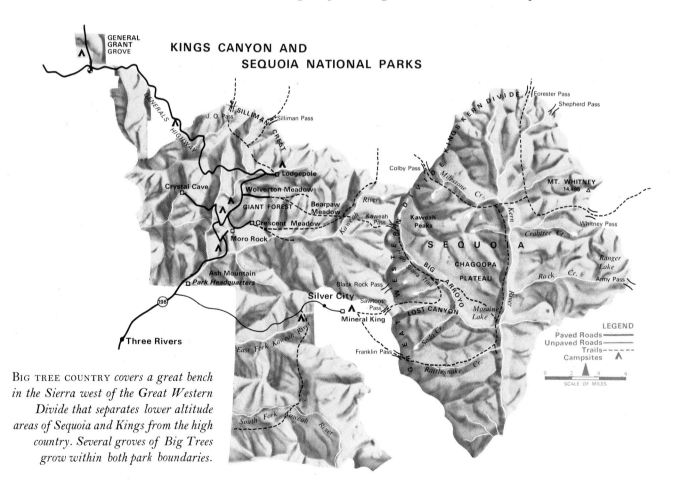

BIG TREE COUNTRY *covers a great bench in the Sierra west of the Great Western Divide that separates lower altitude areas of Sequoia and Kings from the high country. Several groves of Big Trees grow within both park boundaries.*

SIERRA BIG TREE

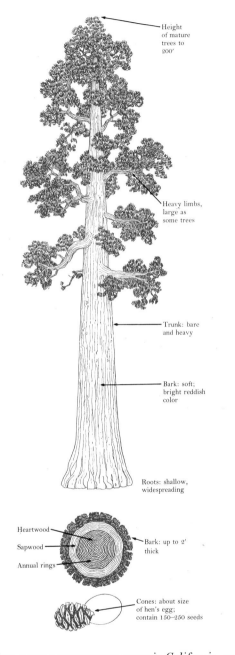

Height of mature trees to 200'

Heavy limbs, large as some trees

Trunk: bare and heavy

Bark: soft; bright reddish color

Roots: shallow, widespreading

Heartwood

Sapwood

Annual rings

Bark: up to 2' thick

Cones: about size of hen's egg; contain 150–250 seeds

Two kinds of redwoods *grow in California, one along the coast, the other in the Sierra. Though not of the same species, the two are often compared. The Big Tree is not so tall as the Coast redwood, but is more massive, has thicker bark and heavier, more angular limbs; its cones are larger, needles scalier.* RIGHT: *General Grant Tree, second-largest in world and the "Nation's Christmas Tree."*

SNOW-STARVED CALIFORNIANS *ascend to Wolverton and Lodgepole to ski, try their blades on the ice rink, or* (RIGHT) *snowshoe through the silent groves at Giant Forest. The main road, kept open all winter, passes through cathedral aisles of white-robed trees, in a world of flawless white where no sound is heard but the crunching of spotless snow under the tires.*

THE THRILL OF HER FIRST SLED *ride lights the face of the little girl, defying gravity on a slick slope. For many children raised in temperate California, the pre-bunny slopes at Sequoia offer the first exciting experience with snow.*

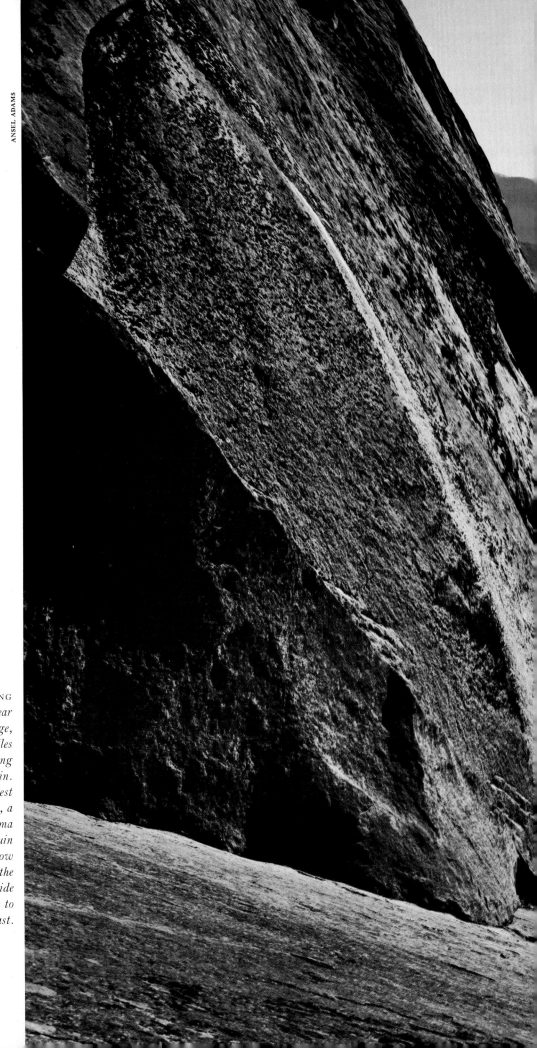

Moro Rock, looming
above the trees near
Giant Forest Village,
can be seen for miles
from the grade leading
up from Ash Mountain.
From its crest
(6,725 ft.), a
360-degree panorama
takes in the San Joaquin
Valley 6,000 feet below
to the west and the
Great Western Divide
7,000 feet above to
the east.

High Country

FOR NINE MONTHS OF THE YEAR, the high country in Sequoia and Kings Canyon National Parks belongs to the native wildlife; during the other three, this roadless domain is a playground for a varied lot of devotees, some hiking alone, some in small groups, and some in organized parties as large as small armies.

The main traffic arterial is the John Muir Trail, which begins in Yosemite Valley and runs south for 225 high-elevation miles to Whitney Portal, about half of its route lying within the boundaries of Kings Canyon and Sequoia parks. This remarkable pathway, which took 40-odd years to complete, was first conceived by the Sierra Club in 1892. Its route was surveyed over several years, construction was begun in 1915, and it was finally finished in 1938. The trail was named in honor of John Muir, who died just before construction was started.

A network of supplementary trails within the two parks gives access to the full variety of High Sierra terrain: cool, silent forests of fir and pine; knife-edged passes; snowbanks; hundreds of lakes; marshy alpine meadows sprinkled with wildflowers; and talus slopes where marmots sun themselves.

EARLY MORNING RISERS *stuff their backpacks with lunches and fishing gear at Bearpaw Meadow camp, located on a breathtaking perch on the shoulder of a deep canyon.*

MOST OF THE TRUE HIGH SIERRA *lies within Kings Canyon and Sequoia national parks. The eastern edge of this high domain runs along the spine of the Sierra block and drops down steeply to the Owens Valley outside the parks' boundary. Several major rivers rise within the drainage basins in the two parks. Main barricade to the west is the 12,000-foot Great Western Divide that isolates this roadless land. A net of trails provides access to almost every corner of the two parks. Main artery is the north-south John Muir Trail; next in importance, the High Sierra Trail from Giant Forest to Mount Whitney.*

BILL JONES

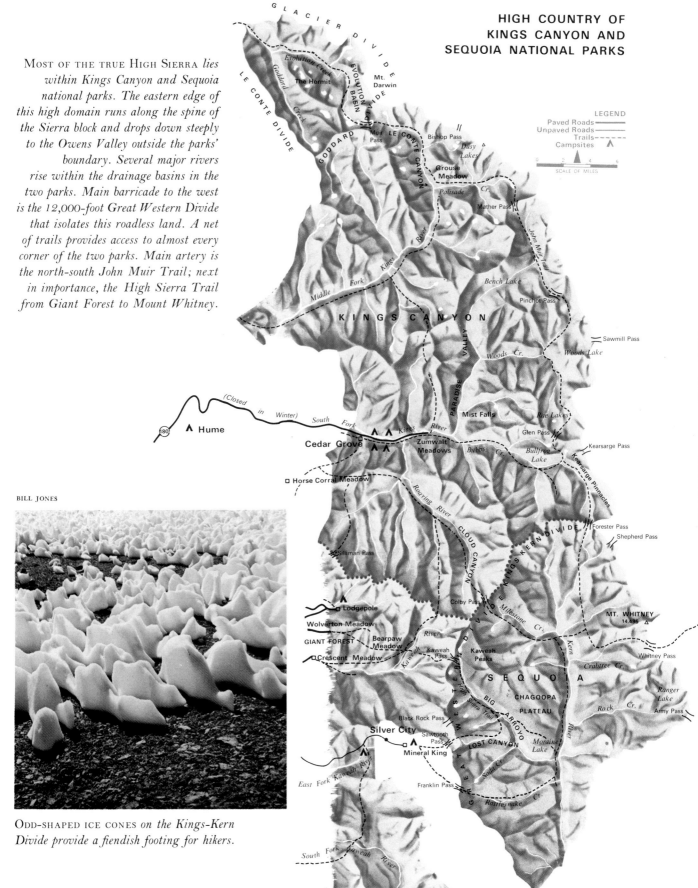

HIGH COUNTRY OF KINGS CANYON AND SEQUOIA NATIONAL PARKS

LEGEND
Paved Roads ━━━━
Unpaved Roads ━━━━
Trails ━━━━
Campsites ⋀

0   2   4   6
SCALE OF MILES

GLACIER DIVIDE

LE CONTE DIVIDE

GODDARD DIVIDE

Evolution Creek
The Hermit
Goddard Creek
Mt. Darwin
EVOLUTION BASIN

Muir Pass
LE CONTE CANYON
Bishop Pass
Dusy Lakes
Grouse Meadow
Palisade Cr.

Kings River
Middle Fork
Palisade
Mather Pass

Bench Lake
Pinchot Pass

John Muir Trail

KINGS CANYON

PARADISE VALLEY

Sawmill Pass

Woods Cr.
Woods Lake

(Closed in Winter)
South Fork
180
⋀ Hume

Mist Falls
Rae Lakes

Kings River
Cedar Grove ⋀⋀
⋀⋀
Zumwalt Meadows
Bubbs Cr.
Glen Pass
Bullfrog Lake
Kearsarge Pass
Kearsarge Pinnacles

◻ Horse Corral Meadow

Roaring River
CLOUD CANYON
KINGS-KERN DIVIDE
Forester Pass
Shepherd Pass

Silliman Pass

Colby Pass
Millstone Cr.
MT. WHITNEY
14,495 △

⋀ Lodgepole
Wolverton Meadow
GIANT FOREST
Bearpaw Meadow
◻ Crescent Meadow

Kaweah River
Kaweah Pass
Kaweah Peaks

SEQUOIA
Kern River
Crabtree Cr.
Whitney Pass

Ranger Lake
CHAGOOPA PLATEAU
Rock Cr.
Army Pass

Black Rock Pass
Silver City ●
◻ ⋀ Sawtooth Pass
Mineral King

High Sierra Trail
BIG ARROYO
LOST CANYON
Moraine Lake

GREAT WESTERN DIVIDE
Soda Cr.

East Fork Kaweah River
Franklin Pass
Rattlesnake Cr.

South Fork Kaweah River

123

ODD-SHAPED ICE CONES *on the Kings-Kern Divide provide a fiendish footing for hikers.*

DAVID MUENCH

FROM THE SUMMIT OF MORO ROCK *a grand winter's scene spreads into view. Snow covers the Great Western Divide to the east, sealing off the barricade to the High Sierra until spring. Framing the view, the pendulous branches of a sugar pine seem to offer benediction. These magnificent trees, with their 18-inch cones, are striking individuals in forests in the 4,500-9,000 foot range. Fire or axe wounds in the wood of a living tree cause it to exude a white, sweet, chewable but cathartic gum that was used by Indians and early settlers.*

IN A DEEP GROOVE *worn by the passage of thousands of hikers and pack animals over the years, the John Muir Trail swings across typical high country just below 12,000-foot Pinchot Pass. Where such trails are located near lakes, streams, and through meadows, they are being relocated to prevent erosion, overgrazing by pack animals, or changes in the ecological balance of alpine meadows.*

FROM THE TOP OF MOUNT WHITNEY, *highest point in the United States outside of Alaska, mountain peaks jut upward in all directions in this view to the northwest across the upper end of the vast Kern River basin. The peak was named in 1871 for J. D. Whitney, leader of the Geologic Survey party that first determined its exact height in 1864. For a brief time, the mountain carried the name Fisherman's Peak. First ascent: 1873.*

EAST-WEST SLICE THROUGH THE SIERRA

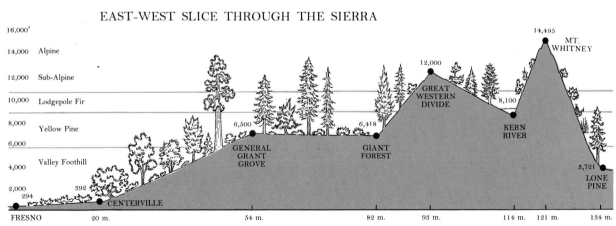

AN EAST-WEST SLICE THROUGH SEQUOIA *reveals the extreme range of altitude, terrain, and tree-cover encompassed within the park's boundaries. In a span of 67 miles the elevation ascends 8,000 feet to the top of Mount Whitney on the eastern border, then drops 11,000 feet in a brief 13 miles.*

LIKE BLEACHERS IN A GIGANTIC STADIUM, *sections of the western slopes of Mount Whitney ascend in a series of stair-like rock formations.*

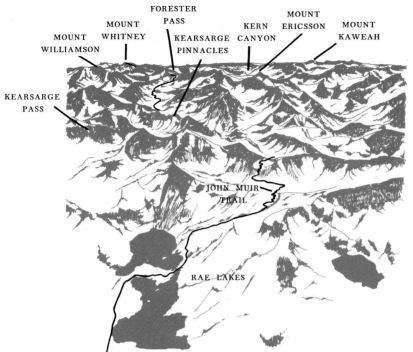

MOUNT WILLIAMSON

MOUNT WHITNEY

FORESTER PASS

KEARSARGE PINNACLES

KERN CANYON

MOUNT ERICSSON

MOUNT KAWEAH

KEARSARGE PASS

JOHN MUIR TRAIL

RAE LAKES

SOUTHERN CLIMAX OF THE JOHN MUIR TRAIL *as viewed from the air. The trail skirts Upper Rae Lake, disappears over Glen Pass, climbs to Forester Pass and thence to the top of Mount Whitney. This is true High Sierra, a seemingly desolate and forbidding expanse of granite cliffs and basins—oppressive to travelers who prefer the friendlier forested mountains lower down—but when viewed close-up, the high country becomes an inviting land of small valleys, hidden forests and meadows, rushing streams and imprisoned lakes, all seen in sharpened contrast to the massive architecture of the great range that rises on all sides.*

FAVORITE TRAIL COMPANION *of many hiking parties, the lowly burro adds a fascinating personality to any group. Yet, as one burro-wise hiker puts it "if the burro doesn't have a good time, you won't either." Their antenna-like ears swing in arcs to pick up unfamiliar sounds, listen to bird songs, or register disapproval of proceedings. Their melodious 5 A.M. reveille launches many a bleary-eyed hiking party on the trail.*

IN A SETTING OF RUGGED GRANDEUR *high above timberline, the John Muir Trail climbs out of treeless Evolution Basin and heads south along the 10,000-foot shoulders of the Sierra spine.*

MANY HIGH SIERRA RIVERS CASCADE *down deep, V-shaped gorges with few open valleys and scant elbow room for hikers. The Middle Fork of the Kings descends in a tumult of foaming cataracts.*

SEQUOIA AND KINGS CANYON **131**

GRAND CANYON

THE STORY OF THE EARTH ITSELF

PARK FACTS: *Location:* Northwestern Arizona. *Discovered:* 1540. *Established:* February 26, 1919. *Size:* 1,100 sq. mi. *Altitude:* 2,000 to 9,000 feet. *Climate:* Progression of climate from that of Mexican desert at Canyon bottom to that of S. Canada at N. Rim. *Season:* S. Rim, all year; N. Rim, mid-May to late-Oct. *Visitors, 1969:* over 2,000,000.

FROM EITHER NORTH OR SOUTH, you approach through rather flat, temperate country full of the familiar, friendly things of field and forest. The land is broken occasionally by picturesque minor gullies. Then, at the sudden edge of the Grand Canyon of the Colorado, you are confronted with one of the most sublime spectacles of this planet. Yet, standing on the brink for the first time, your impulse may be to turn away. It is not any fear of height, nor of the incredible wilderness gap in a land otherwise subdued by civilization. Rather it is disbelief, even saturation with the incredible size of it all.

A little knowledge of the canyon begets a craving for more. A great knowledge of it begets a greater craving for more. When you look into its depths you are looking back some twenty million centuries. Nowhere else can you do so. Nowhere else is geologic history, beginning with the oldest exposed rock on earth, so clear and orderly. When you look into the gorge you look over a bewildering array of plants and animals that in less awesome surroundings need this whole continent to find suitable homes.

Nobody has seen all of the Grand Canyon—and soon it may be too late to try. Human exploitation of the canyon has accelerated rapidly over the past century, and the builders of dams are eager to bend an already reduced Colorado River ever more to their purpose.

"Ours has been the first, and will doubtless be the last, party of whites to visit this profitless locality," reported Lieutenant J. C. Ives, exploring the Grand Canyon region in 1857. Ives was no historian, and he was an even worse prophet. Thirteen men of Coronado's Spanish expeditions had entered the region in 1540, and the captain in command of the party had registered official dismay at the

IT IS 3,000 FEET DOWN *from Toroweap Point just outside the park to the roiling surface of the Colorado River. Visitors on the brink look over a spectacle so immense that no comparison will explain it.*

PHILIP HYDE

133

unbridgeable barrier posed by the chasm. Since Lieutenant Ives' cheerless pronouncement, the canyon has yielded profit in varying degrees to ranchers, miners, prospectors, horse thieves, hermits, and bootleggers, and has been visited by millions of parties of tourists.

In large measure, the Grand Canyon owes the beginnings of its fame as a natural wonder to the explorations of a one-armed major of artillery named John Wesley Powell. In 1869, the dauntless major set out with a small party in four boats to run the length of the Green River and the Colorado as far as the bottom of the Grand Canyon. It was a bucketing ride that cost the major two of his boats and collapsed the nerve of three men in the crew. But he prevailed. He proved the canyon explorable. The accounts of his adventure are still to be read today. River-runners, in fact, use his journals as a guide to their own journeys.

The results of Powell's turbulent dash included widespread publication of accounts of the adventure. These led to greater awareness of the region, and this in turn led to much further exploration of a Southwest that was, before Powell, largely left blank by the mapmakers. Subsequent expeditions by Powell and others achieved two great results: Several branches of natural science found fertile new fields for study, and Powell's enhanced reputation won him the directorship of the fledgling Smithsonian Institution, which he put well on the way to its present eminent station.

This focus of attention also produced great optimism about the immediate tourist value of the Grand Canyon. Around 1880, an ex-miner named John Hance improved upon the Indian trails to some degree and upon the truth to an even greater extent to impress visitors. By the turn of the century there were hotels, tourist camps, orchards, and gardens at various levels all the way down to the river, and several aerial tramways across it. The Santa Fe Railroad built a spur line from Williams to the South Rim in 1901 and the famous El Tovar Hotel 3 years later, but for most operators the optimism proved short lived. The resorts failed, one by one; cable cars rusted in their moorings; the neglected trails disappeared (John Hance's name survives only on a few minor landmarks). For many years, only the Santa Fe and its subsidiary, Fred Harvey, were able to make a go of the tourist business, and the canyon was left mostly to the Indians whose ancestral homes are along its rims, or, in the case of the Havasupai, at the bottom of the great gorge. In time, substantial interests invested in tourism, and the park has for years served as a magnet for tourists from all over the world.

Efforts to preserve the canyon as a national park were begun soon after the establishment of Yellowstone but required 30 years of campaigning to take effect. The first protagonist, Senator Benjamin Harrison of Indiana, introduced a bill in the upper house in 1882 to make the area a national park. It failed. It was not until 1893 that Harrison, as President of the United States, was able to establish the Grand Canyon Forest Preserve, which could be and was exploited by mining and lumber interests. President Theodore Roosevelt took up the cause after his visit in 1903. He established Grand Canyon National Monument in 1908. An act of Congress in 1919 established Grand Canyon National Park.

"WE ARE SWEPT BROADSIDE DOWN, *and are prevented, by the rebounding waters, from striking against the wall . . . We toss about . . . in these billows, and are carried past the danger." Powell wrote in 1869 of such scrapes again and again, and one was captured by his artist, R. A. Muilerse.*

ON JACOB'S LADDER, *a turn-of-the-century party of riders descends toward the river on mule and horseback. The trail is no longer used, and neither are horses, but woman's courage hasn't flagged at all. See page 151.*

ALTHOUGH HANDICAPPED BY THE LOSS OF AN ARM *in the Civil War, ex-artillery major John Wesley Powell daringly led an expedition down the unexplored Colorado River in 4 boats in 1869. Photographed 22 years later, he still looked hale and hearty, ready for further exploits.*

GRAND CANYON 135

FOR CENTURIES BEFORE WHITE MEN CAME *to the Grand Canyon, Indians
lived in its depths and on its rim. One tribe, the Havasupai, still carries on the
traditions of its ancestors relatively undisturbed by the rush of modern life.
They live deep in the canyon on a small oasis where they raise grain, fruit,
and vegetables as they have done since the 12th century. The 200 members of
the nation support themselves with their produce and tend to the needs of the
increasing numbers of vacationers who take the steep trail down.*

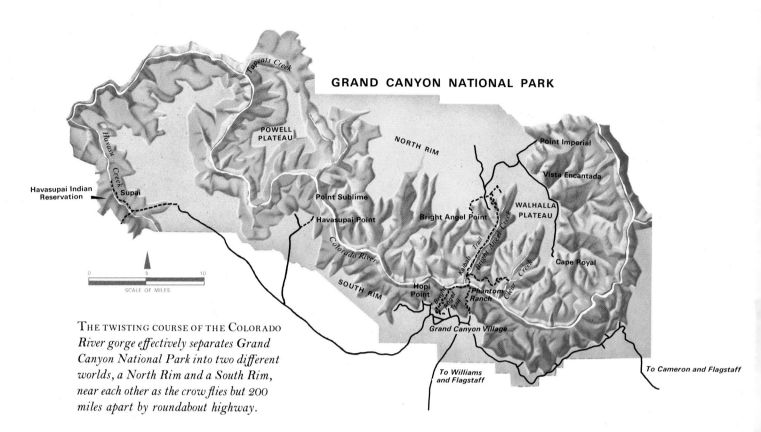

GRAND CANYON NATIONAL PARK

Tapeats Creek

POWELL PLATEAU

NORTH RIM

Point Imperial

Vista Encantada

Point Sublime

WALHALLA PLATEAU

Havasu Creek

Havasupai Indian Reservation

Supai

Havasupai Point

Bright Angel Point

Cape Royal

Colorado River

Kaibab Trail

Bright Angel Creek

Clear Creek

SOUTH RIM

Hopi Point

Bright Angel Trail

Phantom Ranch

Grand Canyon Village

To Williams and Flagstaff

To Cameron and Flagstaff

0   5   10
SCALE OF MILES

THE TWISTING COURSE OF THE COLORADO *River gorge effectively separates Grand Canyon National Park into two different worlds, a North Rim and a South Rim, near each other as the crow flies but 200 miles apart by roundabout highway.*

HOW THE GRAND CANYON WAS FORMED

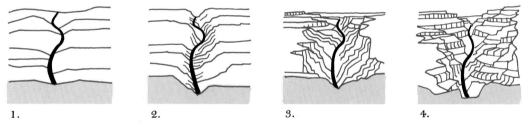

1.   2.   3.   4.

CARVED BY THE SAME FORCES AS A ROADSIDE GULLY, *the Grand Canyon is an awesome example of the work of erosion. 1. First, a lazy river meandered through a gently sloping plain, cutting a shallow channel into the earth. 2. Pressure within the earth slowly tilted the surface, causing the river to run faster, cut deeper. As the channel deepened, land on both sides was gradually eroded into the river and the canyon took on a V shape instead of forming a straight-sided trench. 3. Sides of the V-shaped canyon began to break down as forces of erosion attacked them. Rain sluiced soil down into the canyon bottom where it was carried away by the river. Water from melting snow froze in cracks in rocks, splitting them and further crumbling canyon walls. 4. Over the ages, the river continued to cut deeper, ever following its original configuration, and as it cut, the break-up of the canyon walls became accelerated, disintegrating in an ever-widening gap. In time, the canyon walls will disappear, leaving a flat plain again.*

GRAND CANYON   **137**

GRAND CANYON
History of the Earth

I In the rocks, a billion years.

Possibly, the first spark of life on earth came to be while the rock of the Vishnu Schist formed the surface of this region, instead of the bottom layer of the Grand Canyon.

This black rock of the inner gorge is the oldest man has seen exposed on this planet. Its age is two billion years, an incomprehensibly long span. The youngest rocks in this canyon, only 235 million years old, were deposited as sand by an encroaching sea long before the first dinosaur roamed the land.

The story is written in layers deposited so tidily that geologists use the canyon as a primer. There are missing chapters. Nothing remains of the Ordovician and Silurian geologic periods, which followed the Cambrian, and there is very little left of the Devonian period, which came after the Silurian and before the Carboniferous.

Later chapters are written at Bryce and Zion.

II Down the canyon walls, a continent's range of life.

What is in the rock tells a long story. What is on it does too, in miles rather than time.

A sturdy man can hike down to the bottom of the Grand Canyon and back out again in two days. The experience lets him see plant and animal life that he could also see by walking from Mexico's Sonoran desert to the shore of Hudson's Bay in Canada.

The great depth of the canyon plays tricks with temperatures and precipitation to such a degree that the local range of climate equals the natural range of the entire continent. Mostly, the life zones occur in their logical order; but in some sections, the desert is higher than the Canadian zone, where the canyon's topography makes a high area hot and a lower one cool.

PERMIAN PERIOD
235,000,000 years ago

The highest rim rocks, the Kaibab Limestone, hold fossils of the last trilobites, which swam in a shallow sea. The Coconino Sandstone, a buff layer below, is dune sand. On it walked the early reptiles. Red rocks of the Hermit Shale and Supai Formation are next down, and mark the beginning of the period.

CARBONIFEROUS PERIOD
315,000,000 years ago

Mostly eroded away, these layers represent the time during which the coal of the earth had its beginnings as living plants. The fossil record is slim.

CAMBRIAN PERIOD
550,000,000 years ago

Trilobites dominated a sea floor that was beginning to teem with life, after countless eons struggling up from simple, one-celled beginnings. Top to bottom, the rocks of this period are: Muav Limestone, Bright Angel Shale, Tapeats Sandstone.

PRECAMBRIAN ERA
1,200,000,000 years ago

Longer than all time since, PreCambrian time witnessed somewhere in its dim recesses the first life. Life was earlier than the Grand Canyon Series that ends the era, or than the Chuar Group. It may have begun in the Vishnu Schist that is the bottommost layer known. No fossil remains to tell us what life was like.

BLUE SPRUCE

MT. MAPLE

BLUE GROUSE

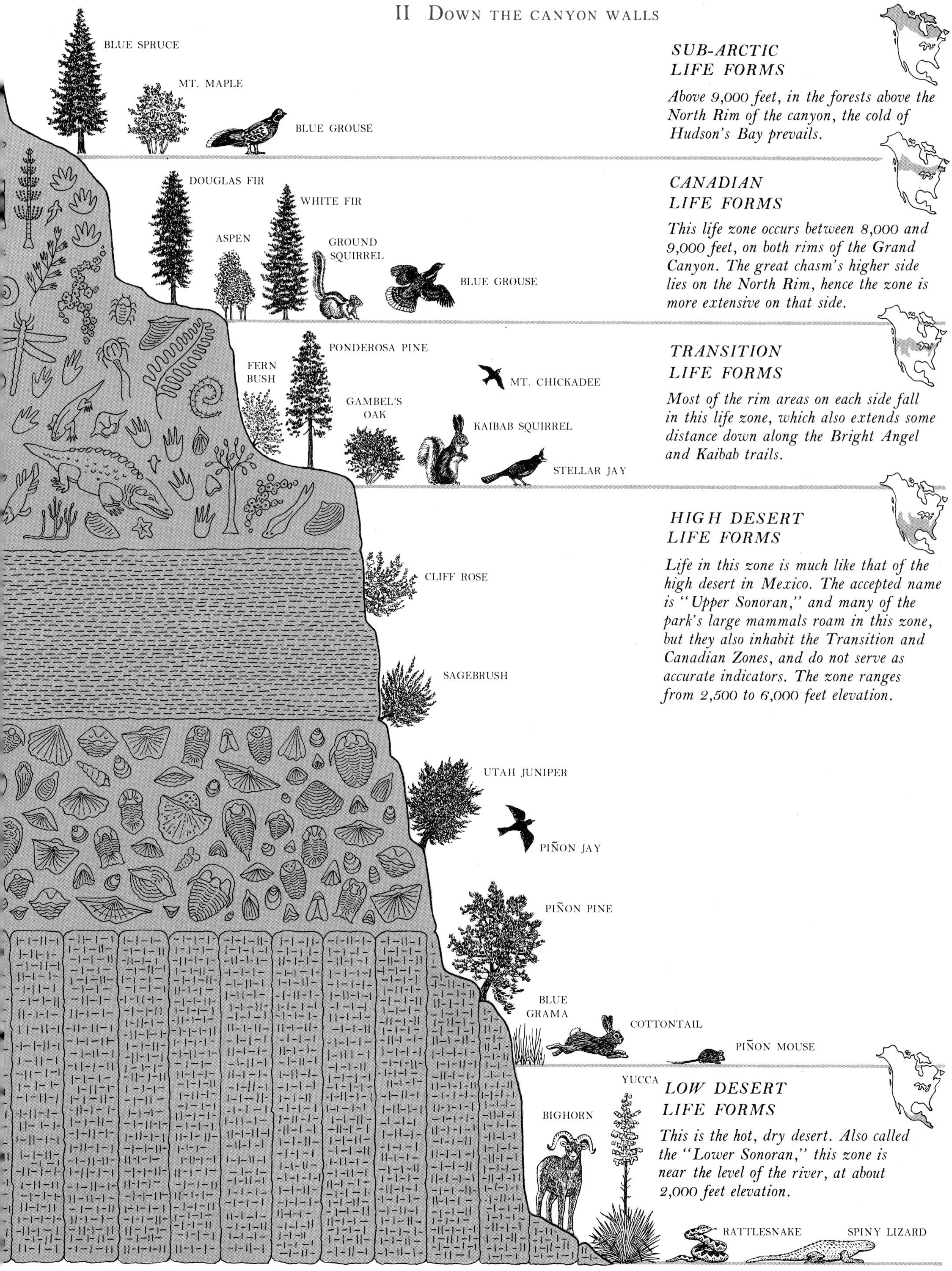

SUB-ARCTIC LIFE FORMS

Above 9,000 feet, in the forests above the North Rim of the canyon, the cold of Hudson's Bay prevails.

DOUGLAS FIR

WHITE FIR

ASPEN

GROUND SQUIRREL

BLUE GROUSE

CANADIAN LIFE FORMS

This life zone occurs between 8,000 and 9,000 feet, on both rims of the Grand Canyon. The great chasm's higher side lies on the North Rim, hence the zone is more extensive on that side.

FERN BUSH

PONDEROSA PINE

MT. CHICKADEE

GAMBEL'S OAK

KAIBAB SQUIRREL

STELLAR JAY

TRANSITION LIFE FORMS

Most of the rim areas on each side fall in this life zone, which also extends some distance down along the Bright Angel and Kaibab trails.

CLIFF ROSE

HIGH DESERT LIFE FORMS

Life in this zone is much like that of the high desert in Mexico. The accepted name is "Upper Sonoran," and many of the park's large mammals roam in this zone, but they also inhabit the Transition and Canadian Zones, and do not serve as accurate indicators. The zone ranges from 2,500 to 6,000 feet elevation.

SAGEBRUSH

UTAH JUNIPER

PIÑON JAY

PIÑON PINE

BLUE GRAMA

COTTONTAIL

PIÑON MOUSE

YUCCA

BIGHORN

LOW DESERT LIFE FORMS

This is the hot, dry desert. Also called the "Lower Sonoran," this zone is near the level of the river, at about 2,000 feet elevation.

RATTLESNAKE

SPINY LIZARD

North Rim

THERE ARE TWO CENTERS OF TOURIST INTEREST in the park—the North Rim and the South Rim of the great canyon. They are a mere 10 miles apart to a crow, or two days' hard hiking to men of stout heart and strong limb, or 215 road miles distant from each other. A great many enchanted visitors prefer to see one rim one year, the other the next.

ON THE NORTH RIM, altitudes run a thousand feet or so higher than on the South Rim. There is a greater variety in nature, and somewhat less diverse evidence of man's hand in the landscape.

Snow falls early and deep on the North Rim. The end of the tourist season is in sight by October, when the aspens put on a great, golden show of color. When the snow flies, as many as 200 inches may blanket the ground by May. Then warming updrafts from the canyon encourage wildflowers to bloom just at the rim. As snowbanks melt before a warming sun, the bright flowers spread ever more widely.

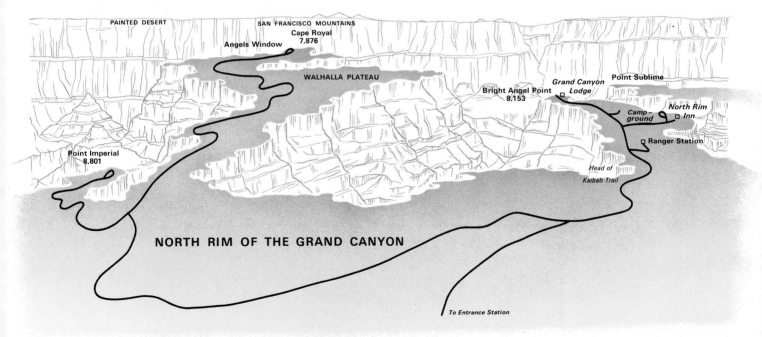

THE ANGELS' WINDOW *is a hole through a thin point of rock projecting into the canyon near Cape Royal, a stark contrast to tranquil woods nearby.*

142 GRAND CANYON

ON THE LOFTY NORTH RIM, FLAMING AUTUMN *colors light the quaking aspens after September. Beyond, for as far as the eye can see, the canyon provides pastel counterpoint to its vivid rim country. The show ends its brief life beneath the first snowy mantle of winter.*

South Rim

"NO MATTER HOW FAR YOU HAVE WANDERED hitherto, or how many famous gorges and valleys you have seen, this one, the Grand Canyon of the Colorado will seem as novel to you, as unearthly in the color and grandeur and quantity of its architecture, as if you had found it after death, on some other star." So wrote John Muir, after he had visited the South Rim in the 1890's, eloquently summarizing the emotional response that this vast spectacle evokes in the traveler when he first sees it.

It is at the South Rim that the great majority of travelers experience this emotional impact. For nearly a century, tourists have converged here to soak in the unbelievable view. Being closer to major population centers and trunk highways than its counterpart across the canyon, the South Rim is easily accessible by bus, plane, or car, and it has always drawn the heavier volume of tourists. As a consequence, it is well provided with facilities for travelers both inside and outside the park: a half dozen hotels, two large campgrounds, information centers, and gift shops bulging with Navajo and Hopi handicrafts.

Crowded as it is in season, the South Rim still offers ample opportunities to view the ever-changing canyon. Numerous turnouts along the rim road permit motorists to drive right to the brink; and for a more intimate view, travelers can stroll along the 2½-mile trail that follows the lip of the canyon. Even in winter, when snow is deep on the ground (the elevation is 7,000 feet) but not on the plowed roads, the rim is accessible and the visitor can enjoy the unforgettable sight of the canyon walls frosted with snow.

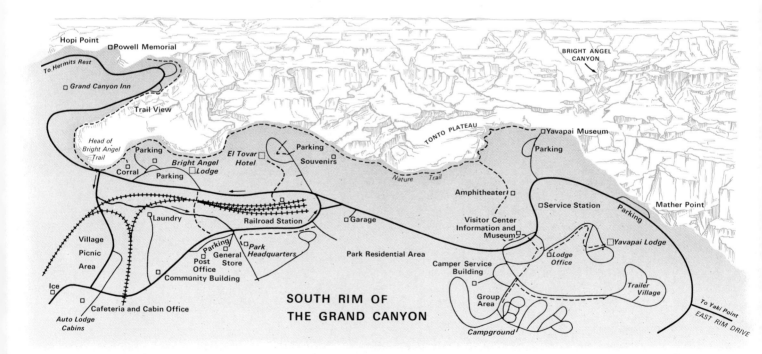

SOUTH RIM OF
THE GRAND CANYON

THE USUAL FIRST LOOK, MATHER POINT, *is where the entrance road first meets the South Rim. Across the chasm, Bright Angel Canyon extends 19 miles northward.*

146　GRAND CANYON

STARK SHAPES AND BRILLIANT COLORS *fill the canyon in an afternoon of intense sunlight. In the softer light of morning the views from the South Rim are colored in the pastel hues of blue, purple, and gold. On a stormy day the colors go dull, even sullen; then, in the mists afterward, a new brightness shines forth.*

ANSEL ADAMS

148   GRAND CANYON

FROM THE NORTH RIM, *looking east, south, and west, William H. Holmes produced this 22-mile panorama for science in 1880, transcending mere diagrams with an eye sensitive to composition.*

FROM POINT IMPERIAL (LEFT), *the camera sees only a fraction of the linear sweep of the South Rim that artist Holmes was able to capture on his drawing board.*

WATCH TOWER *at Desert View offers startlingly long views over the canyon. It is based upon prehistoric watchtowers built by Indians elsewhere in the southwest.*

Inner Canyon

IF YOU PAUSE FOR AN HOUR OR TWO somewhere along the rim and let the Grand Canyon soak into your soul, you will feel some of the lure that turns men into explorers. You will get enough of the big view and will want to get a closer look at the working parts. Sooner or later you will be tugged down one of the trails into the inner canyon.

From either rim, you can hike down or you can ride a mule. At the bottom is a desert, hot and dry and relieved only by the river. It is no place for Sunday strollers to wander aimlessly.

From the South Rim, the mule trips go down the Bright Angel and Kaibab Trails; from the North Rim, they descend the North Kaibab Trail. In summer, the methodical beasts plod their memorized routes in such numbers that a certain air of the barnyard arises from the wide, sun-drenched trails. Users of this service will gain a new appreciation of the width of a mule. Hikers would do well to allow two days to get from the rim to the river and back. Experienced hikers with respect for the effects of heat and dehydration, and with full knowledge of topographic map-reading, may prefer the less traveled Clear Creek, Thunder Spring, or Supai trails.

JOSEPH WAMPLER

A HALF DOZEN DASHING *creeks flow out of tributary canyons. Most issue from the Redwall Limestone, from which many gather the mineral wealth to build high monuments to themselves out of travertine. A welcome by-product to dusty hikers is a natural bathtub safe for swimming, at Havasu.*

IN THE TYPICAL AUTUMN CALM, *as the mule string maintains its methodical pace along memorized zigzags of the Bright Angel or Kaibab trail, you hear above the hoofsteps the jet-like swish of white-throated swifts flying close to the cliffs. You look sometimes out to the panorama of the canyon, sometimes at the edge of the trail to see Indian paintbrush, or gilia, or penstemon thriving where there is soil for a root to cling to. A few novices hike down, ignore the warning signs, and come out on the back of a mournful-looking mule that costs as much as $40 when he is called in for a "drag-out."*

151

CARVING A SINUOUS WAY *through brown Tapeats sandstone, crystal-clear
Deer Creek hastens to its 125-foot fall into the Colorado River.*

FRED HARVEY

MARTIN LITTON

THE ONLY SAFE CROSSING *of the Colorado River is on the
suspension bridge at the bottom of the Kaibab Trail. To see the
river closely, you have to "run" it. No trail stays with it. With
the Glen Canyon Dam operating, it can be run only in certain
seasons. Even at its best, it isn't the test that it once was.*

BRYCE CANYON

A TOUGH PLACE TO FIND A COW

PARK FACTS: *Location:* South central Utah. *Discovered:* 1800's. *Established:* June 7, 1924. *Size: 56* sq. mi. *Altitude:* 6,600 to 9,105 feet. *Climate:* March to November, warm days and cool nights. Winters cold with snow. Air is thin due to high elevation. *Season:* All year; main road kept open in winter. *Visitors, 1968:* 320,800.

THE PAIUTE INDIANS CALLED IT "UNCA-TIMPE-WA-WINCE-POCK-ICH," which means Red-rocks-standing-like-men-in-a-bowl-shaped-canyon. Ebenezer Bryce, the canyon's first resident, had a saltier phrase. In his words, it was "a tough place to find a stray cow." Both descriptions are accurate.

Bryce Canyon is the result of erosive forces. For millions of years, wind, rain, sleet, and frost have worked relentlessly on the multicolored limestone of this great amphitheater. They have shaped countless columns, spires, walled windows, and figures of every description in soft reds, yellows, oranges, greys, and whites. These fantastic forms, filling a huge half-bowl 15 miles across, defy the imagination—or stimulate it, for here is an astonishing variety of shapes, some grotesque, some beautiful.

Just as the forces of nature created the landscape, so do the vagaries of the day alter it for the viewer. The domes and temples and spires never seem twice the same. With every cloud shadow, with every change of light, with every summer shower, the scene is new, and newly exciting. No matter how familiar one may be with this fairyland of form and color, some new formation or some undetected tone is always to be discovered.

It is possible, if you wish, to see Bryce Canyon National Park by car. A paved road skirts the western rim for 20 miles, terminating at Rainbow Point. You can look into a dozen minor amphitheaters, each with a character of its own. From Rainbow Point unfolds a sweeping view not only of the canyon but of the country beyond. On a clear day you can see the Henry Mountains, 90 miles away, the Tushars, 60 miles to the north, and, 80 miles to the southeast on the Arizona border, Navajo Mountain, sacred as the home of their war god.

"THE WILDEST AND MOST WONDERFUL SCENE that the eye of man ever beheld," is the way an enraptured surveyor described the eroded fantasy of the Pink Cliffs in 1876. But early settlers were not so bemused: they considered this a hostile place for raising crops or grazing cattle.

ANSEL ADAMS

155

But to experience the park adequately, to capture its true grandeur and its varied moods, walk or ride into its heart over one of the fine trails, only in this way can you appreciate the beauty of the formations. The trails vary in length, from 1½ to 8 miles, and in gradient from nearly level to steep (those that lead into the canyon itself).

The colorful formations are geologically young—a mere million years of age. They overlie more ancient rocks of the strata exposed today in the walls of Zion Canyon to the west and Grand Canyon to the south. Thus one can trace a fascinating sequence in earth history from the oldest rocks of Grand Canyon, through the more recent walls of Zion, to the comparatively young strata of Bryce Canyon.

Bryce is an all-year park, and although access to some sections is limited, the road to certain of the major points is kept open throughout the winter. The beauty of the spires and minarets is no less breathtaking when the delicate colors stand out in contrast to a blanket of snow and frost.

Bryce has been a tourist destination only since the automobile made access possible. Before then, the area was familiar only to trappers and farmers, and before them, to the Indians, who lived in nearby caves or entered the canyon to hunt or to gather herbs, seeds, and berries. Trappers visited the locality in the early 1800's, Mormon scouts explored it between 1850 and 1870, and the first awe-struck descriptions of the fantastic landscape came from geologists and surveyors who explored the canyon in the 1870's. The first settler, Ebenezer Bryce, for whom the park is named, pastured cattle in the labyrinth from 1875 to 1880. Small settlements grew up nearby, but the area was too remote from railroads and wagon routes to grow. It was not until the first automobiles began to push their way through the sands after 1915 that the area gained recognition as a potential park. It was made a national monument in 1923 and a year later was established as Utah National Park, a name that was changed to the present one in 1928.

HOW THE ERODED FANTASY WAS FORMED

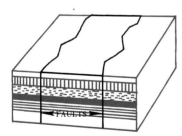 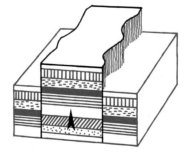 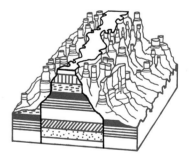

1. DEEP FAULTS FORM IN EARTH'S *crust made of layers of silt, sand, and lime deposited under an ancient inland sea.*

2. MASSIVE PRESSURE FROM BELOW *slowly forces up block of earth between major faults and forms flat-topped mesa.*

3. RAIN, WIND, AND FROST ACTION *gradually wear away edges of mesa; differences in layers produce odd shapes.*

ROBERT COX

WHO ARE THESE? *Viewed close-up, the forms seem to take on identities. Left to right: two-faced Janus; Nebuchadnezzar, with crown, mustache, beard; caped Florence Nightingale; and King Neptune.*

"The stunningest thing out of a *picture, a perfect wilderness of red pinnacles,"* noted the member of a *scientific survey team in 1872. The Pink Cliffs, still considered the finest of Utah's eroded landscapes, stretch for 30 miles along the eastern edge of the Paunsaugunt ("home of the beaver") Plateau. The bright colors, fused into the native rock, are derived from iron—the more iron content the deeper the red. Bands of different colored and textured rock are layers of ancient sands compressed into rock by the immense weight of the thick layer of earth that once covered them but has long since eroded away. Within the brightly colored cliffs are bones of dinosaurs and other fossils of the Age of Reptiles.*

DAVID MUENCH

159

Queen Victoria holds court, *surrounded by her entourage of nobles and ladies-in-waiting. The grotesque figures are the work of wind and rain, shaping stone of varying degrees of hardness. In time (an eon or two), these forces will wear down the jumbled land into a smooth plain.*

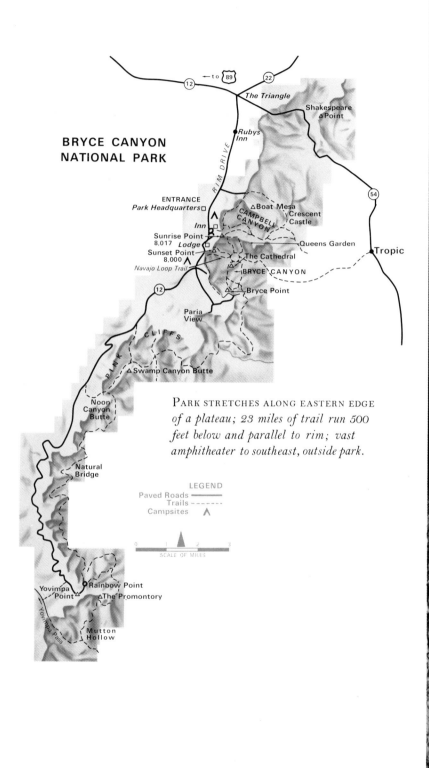

BRYCE CANYON NATIONAL PARK

PARK STRETCHES ALONG EASTERN EDGE *of a plateau; 23 miles of trail run 500 feet below and parallel to rim; vast amphitheater to southeast, outside park.*

LEGEND
Paved Roads ━━━━━
Trails ━ ━ ━ ━ ━
Campsites ⋀

0 1 2 3
SCALE OF MILES

LONE DOUGLAS FIR *started against great odds in semi-darkness, now flourishes, its crown in the sunshine above, where the narrow cleft in the rocks widens out. Located on Navajo Loop Trail, it passes through Wall Street.*

BRYCE CANYON **161**

DAVID MUENCH

DAVID MUENCH

MIXED IN WITH THE *eroded landforms is a pygmy forest of trees and shrubs that grow in poor soil, need little water. Juniper, piñons, and stray yellow pine share a precarious footing with manzanita, mountain mahogany, squaw bush, service berry, and other low growing shrubs. In cool canyons, cottonwoods, maples, birches, and willows grow. Here at Queens Garden sparse forest softens harshness of spectacular cliffs.*

SNOWSHOES WOULD BE NEEDED *for the hike down the Navajo Trail in winter. Snow piles deep on the rim by mid-December and covers the ledges of the Pink Cliffs, brightening the warm-hued filigree with contrasting white. Though accommodations are closed, roads are open to main view points.*

ANSEL ADAMS

ZION

"YOSEMITE VALLEY IN COLOR"

PARK FACTS: *Location:* Southwestern Utah. *Discovered:* 1776. *Established:* November 19, 1919. *Size:* 230 sq. mi. *Altitude:* 3,950 to 8,740 feet. *Climate:* Warm summers, mild winters. Temperature range from 0° to 115°. *Season:* All year. Facilities closed but main road open in snowy months. *Visitors in 1969:* 892,146.

ZION CANYON IS A COLORFUL JEWEL set in a land famed for color. It is a serene canyon, majestic with sandstone cliffs which at times rise more than 3,000 feet above its floor. Without the color—the delicate pinks and reds and whites of the sandstone and the fresh green of the cottonwoods, ash, and maples that border the river—these walls and domes might be overpoweringly stern. But the color softens the scene and casts a special aura over the canyon.

Zion has been called a Yosemite done in oils, for without color the sheer cliffs would resemble the California park in many ways. Zion Canyon is a narrow, curving gorge, 8¾ miles long; the upper end is so narrow that two men standing abreast can touch both walls with their outstretched arms. The canyon is cut by the Virgin River, a Jekyll-and-Hyde sort of stream that is usually clear and peaceful, reflecting the cliffs in its calm pools. But a storm in the higher country can transform it into a relentless torrent, tearing savagely at its banks, and carrying boulders and trees like pebbles and twigs.

Such storms are not frequent, but when they come they have their rewarding aspects. Visitors present at such a time will marvel at the power of the river and perhaps be loath to turn their eyes from the racing waters. But during a hard rain, a look up the walls of the canyon reveals waterfalls springing to life and plunging over the usually dry cliffs, some dropping 2,000 feet in a single leap. More than 50 large waterfalls and hundreds of smaller ones have been counted at one time during a heavy rain. It has been estimated that each year the Virgin carries three million tons of sediment from the park—an average of 180 carloads each day. Thus the river works as it has worked for centuries, cutting the canyon deeper and deeper through the strata of stone.

GREAT WHITE THRONE, *towering 2,400 feet above the canyon floor, is most majestic of the assembly of blocky peaks that form walls of Zion Canyon. Shading upward from red at base through pink to white, the monolith is crowned with forest.*

165

An excellent road traverses the canyon along the bank of the river and terminates at the Temple of Sinawava. Glorious in daylight hours, the Temple is even more impressive in the soft light of the moon.

There are many good trails, some that penetrate delightful side canyons and others, more strenuous, that climb to the rim on either side. One of the most popular and beautiful is the mile-long walk along the river beginning at the Temple of Sinawava and ending at the entrance to The Narrows. Here the trail passes the Hanging Gardens, where water trickles down the wall to moisten the flowers, ferns, and vines that trail from cracks in the rock.

Zion is an all-year park and each season has its own charm. Spring is fresh with flowers and new foliage. During the hot summer the park is its busiest. In autumn the trees glow brilliantly and tongues of red and yellow flame seem to creep up the ravines. Winter snows seldom linger in the lower part of the canyon, but in the upper portions, a fresh fall converts the landscape into a white fairyland.

Zion was for many years a retreat and a place of special reverence for the Mormon pioneers, who discovered the canyon and named the region "Zion," meaning "the heavenly city of God," and bestowed religious names on many of the rock formations. The area had been originally discovered by Spanish padres in 1776, explored 50 years later by Jedediah Smith and his fur-trappers, and then developed by the Mormons a decade after the founding of Salt Lake City in 1847. The area was not set aside for public use until 1909, when it was designated Mukuntuweap National Monument. Ten years later it was enlarged and changed to Zion National Park.

WILLIAM L. VAN ALLEN

ROCKY MOUNTAIN MULE DEER *come out of the side canyons in late afternoon to feed in the river valleys.*

QUIET-RUNNING VIRGIN RIVER
becomes a raging torrent when cloudbursts swell it to flood stage. Named by explorer Jedediah Smith in 1827 for Thomas Virgin.

WEEPING ROCK *sheds its tears on visitors who step into cave behind falling water. Surface water on rim seeps down through porous cliffs and emerges as curtain of falling drops. Seepage is evident throughout the park and dozens of waterfalls spring to life after each rain.*

THE WATER OUZEL

Water ouzels live along the river, fly in and out of the water, swimming and walking under surface in search of food.

COLOR IN THE CLIFFS *is in the rock itself, in the vegetation, surface stains, and lichens. Hues change with the hour as sun shifts, are intensified or fused with other colors when reflections from nearby peaks are set aglow by the sun, and look their best after a rain. Dominant color is red, derived from iron and magnesium in the sandstone.*

ANSEL ADAMS

FROM JOHN MUIR'S "MOUNTAINS OF CALIFORNIA," 1894

LIKE A HUGE TOPOGRAPHIC MAP, *contour lines of ancient sand dunes are solidified into a massive stairway on eastern edge of the park, just off highway.*

ZION NATIONAL PARK

LEGEND

Paved Roads ————
Unimproved Roads ————
Trails ··········
Campsites ⋀

SCALE OF MILES

HORSE RANCH
8,740 △

NAGUNT
MESA △
TIMBER TOP
△8,075
Kolob Arch

LAVA
POINT
7,890 △

POCKET
MESA

HORSE PASTURE PLATEAU

Potato
Hollow

Sleepy
Hollow

The Narrows

GREATHEART
MESA

Temple of Sinawava
6411

△ Inclined Temple

Echo
Canyon

GREAT WEST CANYON

△ Great White Throne

□ Zion Lodge

ZION CANYON

Virgin River

The Beehives △

△ Mountain of the Sun

Visitor Center

EAST
ENTRANCE

West Temple △

□ Zion Inn

CHECKERBOARD
MESA

SOUTH ENTRANCE
3450

Petrified
Forest

North Fork Virgin River

● Springdale

PARUNUWEAP CANYON

15 Virgin ●

Grafton ●

Rockville ●

170 ZION

So TORTURED IS THE ZION TERRAIN *that it was not completely mapped until 1930, when it was systematically photographed from the air.*

CRISS-CROSS CREVICING *of the sandstone in Checkerboard Mesa, near the east entrance, presents a striking linear pattern. Cracks run both vertically and horizontally, slicing the rock into great blocks and making the stone vulnerable to erosion. Water seeps down the crevices, slowly dissolving soluble sandstone, and in winter when it freezes, it widens the cracks by fracturing the rock along edge.*

RAY ATKESON

CANYONLANDS

"MORE STANDING UP LAND THAN LAYING DOWN"

PARK FACTS: *Location:* Southeastern Utah. *Discovered:* early 1800's. *Established:* September 12, 1964. *Size:* 402 sq. mi. *Altitude:* 3,800-6,000 ft. *Climate:* Hot in summer, likely to be very cold in winter. *Season:* All year. *Visitors in 1968:* 26,000.

CONTAINING "THE MOST VARIED and spectacular examples of erosion in the world," Canyonlands National Park protects a wild array of arches, needles, spires, crenelated mesas, and standing rocks.

The geologic fantasies are the end-product of some 20 million years of erosional shaping by two abrasive rivers, the Green and the Colorado, abetted by wind and rain and frost. The multicolored stone is sculptured according to the resistance of its varying layers to the forces of erosion, thereby creating the oddly striped and chiseled abstractions that astound or humble the viewer. The strange forms have stirred men to imaginative namings, such as, The Golden Stairs, Elephant Canyon, Island in the Sky, Tapestry Slab, Devils Lane, and Paul Bunyans Potty.

Unlike the narrow, mile-wide chasm of the Grand Canyon downriver, the outer walls of this vast area are a hundred miles apart and the great trough in between is filled with geological oddities that will in another 10 or 20 million years be eroded to flat desert floor.

The park is a wilderness, penetrable only on foot or horseback or in a four-wheel-drive vehicle. Trails and jeep roads skirt the rim of the high plateaus, plunge down the steep canyon walls (one descent is 40 per cent), and wander in and out among the eerie formations rising from the canyon floors. Travelers may enter the park by one of two entrances, but leave their cars at established parking areas, for the average family automobile is no match for these rough pathways.

Although the park is open all year to visitors, travelers must be prepared for climatic extremes that range from temperatures of mid-90's in summer to 20° or less in winter. There are no accommodations within the park, except for simple campgrounds, but motels and resorts are just outside the park.

A DEEP GORGE CHEWED *out of the sandstone by the Colorado River is rimmed by peculiar, rectangular shaped rock walls, squared off by erosion and weathering. These forms are found in the Standing Rocks section of Monument Basin.*

PHILIP HYDE

173

TOUR GROUP PAUSES *for lunch under*
hanging rock just outside Chesler Park.
In the background can be seen the striking
figurations of the rugged Needles Country.

**CANYONLANDS
NATIONAL PARK**

COVERING THREE LEVELS, *the park divides into:*
Island in the Sky, a high mesa with an elevation of 6,000
feet, that is surrounded by a mezzanine, the 4,400-foot
high White Rim, which in turn overlooks the flat river
valleys 500 feet below. Passenger cars can approach only
to Grandview or Dead Horse Point. From Elephant Hill,
the going is by foot, horse, trailbike, or jeep.

THE TORTUOUS COLORADO RIVER *cuts a twisting gorge*
through the park. One spectacular convolution, where
it nearly crosses its own path, can best be viewed from
Dead Horse Point, just outside the park boundary.

DAVID MUENCH

Map labels:

To Moab and 160
SCENIC HIGHWAY
Mineral Bottom
Potash Mine
Ranger Station
Shafer Trail
The Neck
Upheaval Dome
ISLAND IN THE SKY
WHITE RIM
Green River Overlook
Mesa Trail
Anderson Bottom
WHITE RIM
Green River
Grandview Point 6,100
Monument Basin
Junction Butte
THE MAZE
River
River
Colorado River
LAND OF STANDING ROCKS
Lower Jump
Candlestick Spire
Confluence Overlook
Ranger Station
To Monticello and 160
Spanish Bottom
Silver Stairs
Squaw Butte
Squaw Flat
North Six-Shooter Peak 6,374
GLEN CANYON RECREATION AREA
The Grabens
CYCLONE CANYON
Devils Lane
ELEPHANT CANYON
Elephant Hill
THE NEEDLES
CATARACT CANYON
Colorado River
Virginia Park
Tower Ruin
Druid Arch
HORSE CANYON
South Six-Shooter Peak 6,132
Angel Arch
Upper Jump
All American Man
Big Ruin

LEGEND
Campsites ∧
Unimproved Roads
Jeep Roads
Trails

0 1 2 3 4 5
SCALE IN MILES

PETRIFIED FOREST

ALCHEMY IN THE DESERT

PARK FACTS: *Location:* Eastern Arizona. *Discovered:* 1851. *Established:* Put under Forest Preserve, 1896; made national monument, 1906; national park, December 9, 1962. *Size:* 147 sq. mi. *Altitude:* 5,300 to 6,235 feet. *Climate:* Area receives less than 10 inches of moisture per year. *Season:* All year. *Visitors in 1969:* 1,000,000.

THE FASCINATION OF PETRIFIED WOOD seems almost universal. Its attraction is more than a matter of beauty; it is partly the mystery of a magic transformation.

Mineralized wood is found in many places, but nowhere in such abundance as on the high plateau of northeastern Arizona. There, in six concentrations, great logs of jasper and agate are interspersed with smaller sections and fragments that glisten in the sun like a ground cover of gems.

Explorers reported these "stone trees" in 1851, but it was another 30 years before there were enough settlers and travelers to affect the area seriously. Then the depredations of souvenir hunters and commercial exploiters reached the point where great quantities of petrified wood were being carried off. Logs were blasted in search of the amethysts that some contained; a stamp mill was even erected nearby to crush the trees into abrasives.

The aroused citizens of Arizona, through the territorial legislature, finally won federal protection for the area, and in 1906 the Petrified Forest National Monument was established. In 1962 it was designated a national park.

Petrified wood is manufactured by nature under rather special circumstances. The mineralized logs started as living trees in a prehistoric forest. When they died and fell, they were washed down from the hills by flood waters and covered, before they could decay, with sand, mud, and volcanic ash. Eventually some geologic upheaval lifted the land, and wind and rain began to wear away the overlying sediments. After millions of years, the trees were exposed. But the wood had been replaced, cell by cell, by silica borne in the water filtering down through the overlying strata. Oxides of iron and magnesium, carried in the same water, gave the logs the red, green, and black hues we see today.

THE PROFILE OF BLUE MESA *changes little by little as wind and rain erode it. Petrified logs cap small ridges until they are undercut and fall all a-tumble. As the old ridges crumble, new ones begin beneath the fallen log fragments.*

DARWIN VAN CAMPEN

ON AGATE BRIDGE *a stroller of 1899 takes a wonder of nature in stride.*
Soft sandstone eroded to form the 40-foot log bridge, which is still intact.

The concentrations of petrified wood are the prime attractions at this national park, but there are other reasons to visit. One is the Painted Desert. This great expanse of colored sand stretches for many miles across northern Arizona, and a splendid sampling is included within the park boundaries. The colors are richest after a rain, but they are impressive in any light, and they change in tone and intensity as the day passes. A rim road, with parking areas at the best viewing points, skirts this portion of the park.

The main road through the stone forests also takes you past Puerco Indian Ruin, the remains of an ancient pueblo occupied until about 600 years ago, and Newspaper Rock, a great block of sandstone inscribed with petroglyphs. Another partially restored pueblo, Agate House, can be reached by trail from the Rainbow Forest parking area.

TREES THAT FELL *200,000,000 years ago are preserved*
by silica, to the interest of scientists, and dyed beautifully
by iron oxide and magnesium, to the delight of all.

DAVID MUENCH

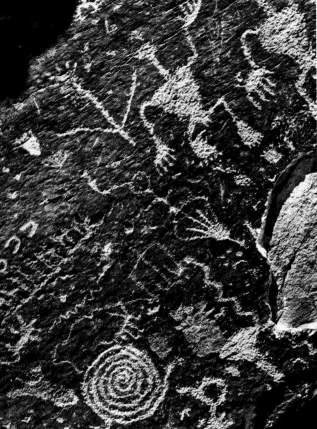

INDIANS KNEW THIS AREA *long before advent of white explorers. Their notes on Newspaper Rock can't be read today, but these petroglyphs may have had religious significance, have been clan symbols or simply "doodles."*

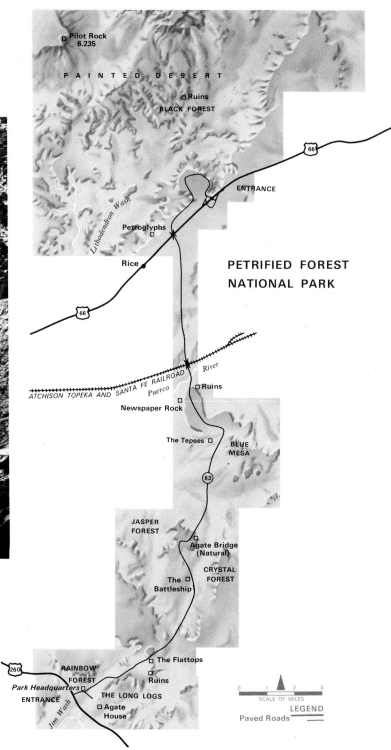

Pilot Rock
6,235

PAINTED DESERT

□ Ruins
BLACK FOREST

66

ENTRANCE

Lithodendron Wash

Petroglyphs ✕

Rice ●

PETRIFIED FOREST
NATIONAL PARK

66

ATCHISON TOPEKA AND SANTA FE RAILROAD   River

Puerco   □ Ruins

□
Newspaper Rock

The Tepees □   BLUE
MESA

63

JASPER
FOREST

□ Agate Bridge
(Natural)

CRYSTAL
FOREST

The □
Battleship

□ The Flattops

260   RAINBOW
FOREST   □ Ruins

Park Headquarters □   THE LONG LOGS
ENTRANCE
Jim Wash   □ Agate
House

0   1   2   3
SCALE OF MILES

LEGEND
Paved Roads

SIX SEPARATE CONCENTRATIONS *of petrified wood flank the 27-mile-long road through the neck of the park. At its north end, the Painted Desert duplicates in sandstone the fiery colors of petrified wood.*

IN THE CRYSTAL FOREST, *soft sandstone is weathering away from beneath a huge petrified log. The long section will fall and break, slowly by man's clock, rapidly by nature's.*

THE FOREST LOOKED LIKE THIS *when the trees were living in the Triassic Period. The globe-topped trees, related to pines, are called* Araucarioxylon. *They dominate the petrified forest.*

PETRIFIED FOREST **181**

MESA VERDE

AMERICA'S OLDEST ABANDONED APARTMENTS

PARK FACTS: *Location:* Southwestern Colorado. *Discovered:* Area discovered by Spanish 1765; Indian dwellings first discovered in 1870's. *Established:* June 29, 1906. *Size:* 80 sq. mi. Estimates indicate more than 500 dwellings within park boundaries. *Altitude:* 6,964 to 8,572 feet. *Season:* All year. *Visitors, 1968:* 449,800.

AFTER A MILLENIUM OF REMARKABLE PROGRESS, the people of the Mesa Verde gave up in A.D. 1300 and moved away. They dissolved a sophisticated culture without learning to write the record. And the question is unanswered after 700 years: Why did they go?

They had come as nomadic hunters in the time of Christ. Within two centuries they had learned to raise corn, and to weave with such consummate skill that they are known to history as the Basket-maker People.

They became the earliest of the pueblo Indians when they learned to cover their storage-pit homes on cave floors with crude huts of logs plastered over with adobe. By A.D. 750 they had come up out of the canyons to the mesa top, where they built connecting rows of rooms close to their farm fields. These were forerunners to the remarkable cliff dwellings. And they had turned from baskets to pottery, which has artistic merit today. They were outstandingly successful farmers.

Some archaeologists think their success was their ruin as well, that their wealth attracted raiders from hostile tribes. They say the evidence points to a retreat return to the cliff caves from which they had started, and not a willing move from the mesa. Whatever the reason, the people continued to farm on the mesa top while they cultivated their skills as masons on those incredibly difficult sites.

An average life span was 30 years; a man worked from the time he was 12 until he was too old at 25. He learned to haul talus up from the bottom of the cliffs and to lay the rock in careful courses, with a minimum of adobe mortar. He learned to string beams of piñon pine to make roofs. He learned to slope walls inward so he could build to a height of four stories. He figured out com-

TO THE NARROW LEDGES ON WHICH THEY BUILT, *the Mesa Verde Indians hauled thousands of stones gathered from talus at the bottoms of the cliffs, and they felled and dragged hundreds of piñon pines to serve as roof beams. They did it all in places chosen because they were difficult to reach, as Square Tower House shows.*

183

DAVID MUENCH

FAR BELOW THE MESA TOP (ABOVE), *Mancos Valley of southwestern Colorado spreads flat and open. The peaceful Indians who farmed on mesa's 2,000-foot height chose remote areas because it was easily defended. Cliff Palace* (LEFT), *more than 700 years after abandonment, remains a most impressive monument to the skills of its builders, who continually added to it during 200 years of occupation. Peak population: about 400.*

plicated ventilating systems for the underground ceremonial room called the kiva, so he could use fire in his ceremonies without choking on the smoke.

While he was mastering these skills, he lived in a society with complex religious practices, a diverse agricultural knowledge, and a trading system that brought goods from as far away as the coast of southern California and the gulfs of Mexico and California.

Then, in about A.D. 1300, it all ended. The land may have worn out. Drought may have come. Enemies may have become too powerful. The social order may have broken down. The cause may have been a combination of all these. Whatever it was, the results were permanent.

The untenanted ruins endure in Mesa Verde National Park. From May 15 to October 15 ranger-guides conduct tours of some of the outstanding ruins. During the remainder of the year, visitors can look down into the great villages and the small ones from vantage points along the roads on the mesa. A great many artifacts were discovered by members of the ranching Wetherill family in 1888 and before the area became a park in 1906. A representative collection is in the fine park museum.

Hiking is not encouraged at Mesa Verde; there are only a few short trails. The campgrounds near the park headquarters operate from May 1 to about October 15.

MESA VERDE   **185**

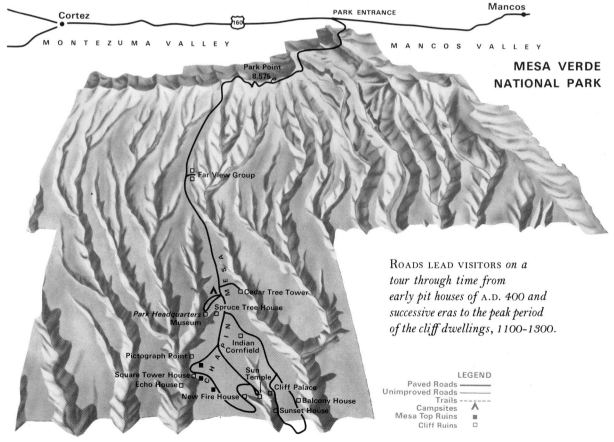

Cortez   PARK ENTRANCE   Mancos

160

M O N T E Z U M A   V A L L E Y   M A N C O S   V A L L E Y

Park Point
8,575

**MESA VERDE
NATIONAL PARK**

Far View Group

M
E
S
A

Cedar Tree Tower

Spruce Tree House

Park Headquarters
Museum

Indian
Cornfield

Pictograph Point

C
H
A
P
I
N

Square Tower House

Sun
Temple

Echo House

Cliff Palace

New Fire House

Balcony House

Sunset House

Roads lead visitors *on a
tour through time from
early pit houses of* A.D. 400 *and
successive eras to the peak period
of the cliff dwellings, 1100-1300.*

LEGEND
Paved Roads ————
Unimproved Roads ⋯⋯⋯⋯
Trails - - - - - -
Campsites ⋏
Mesa Top Ruins ■
Cliff Ruins □

BALCONY HOUSE, *not as large as Cliff Palace, shows signs of even finer workmanship. Cantilevered "porches" were for access and extra storage at upper levels.*

PIT HOUSES WERE FIRST *attempts at construction by the Mesa Verdes. The rude huts covered storage pits and apparently inspired the later ceremonial room called the kiva. Their sites were eventually covered by the cliff dwellings.*

PIT HOUSES

KIVAS WERE USUALLY *circular at Mesa Verde. They were used by the men, who banded together in what probably were fraternal-religious groups. Kivas were the outer rim of the large villages. Their massive walls helped form defensive barriers.*

MYSTERIOUS SUN TEMPLE (*a name of none but poetic significance*) *sits atop mesa. It was built long after Mesa Verde Indians had retreated to cliff caves, and its purpose was probably religious. Nobody knows its exact function, but the D-shaped building is a maze of rooms and corridors. Small dwellings in canyon below could not have supplied enough people to build it. Archaeologists think many family groups shared in its construction; it was never completed.*

MESA VERDE INDIANS MASTERED POTTERY *before they excelled at architecture. These pieces might have been made before the move from the mesa top or might have been fashioned by the village women while their men built the cliff dwellings. Artisans formed the pieces with spiral coils of clay, smoothing the surfaces with extra clay and finger pressure. Black paint is an iron oxide gathered by crushing a commonly found pebble to fine dust. The pieces were fired in nearly smothered ovens. Dippers ranged from 8 to 10 inches long. The double mug is slightly more than 10 inches wide. Pitchers ranged from 8 to 10 inches tall; mugs were in the 3 to 7-inch size. Water jugs (and the effigy figure of the dog) were usually more than a foot tall. Bowls were 6 to 9 inches in diameter.*

MESA VERDE BLACK-ON-WHITE POTTERY

Double Mug

Pitcher

Mug

Dipper

Bowl

Dipper Bowl

Storage Jar

Jug Dog

FOR ONE GIDDY MOMENT, *contemporary visitors to the cliff dwellings can experience life as the original inhabitants lived it. They must climb a long ladder into Balcony House.*

MESA VERDE **189**

CARLSBAD CAVERNS

FANTASY BENEATH THE DESERT

PARK FACTS: *Location:* Southeastern New Mexico. *Discovered:* Settlers knew of caves in 1880's. *Established:* Nat. mon., 1923; nat. park, May 14, 1930. *Size:* 77 sq. mi. Explored caverns cover 13 mi.; 3 mi. open to public. *Altitude:* 4,400 ft. at surface. *Climate:* Surface temps. from 0° to 100°. *Season:* All year. *Visitors, 1968:* 668,401.

AN INFINITY IN TIME AND THE INFINITE POWER of trickling water have hollowed scores of caverns out of the limestone beneath the southeast corner of New Mexico. During the latter part of the 60 million years this has been going on, oozing drops have left mineral trails behind them in the myriad rock sculptures that give the Carlsbad Caverns, the largest of all these caves, their eerie charm.

Nobody knows how extensive these caverns are. More than 13 miles have been explored, at depths ranging down to 1,100 feet below the surface. As many as 5 million bats have shared one mile of cavern. At present, only three of the most amazing miles are open to park visitors.

The easily walked tour trail passes through great vaults with names like Green Lake Room, King's Palace, and Queen's Chamber, where the rock formations support even more picturesque names: Iceberg, Bone Yard, Totem Pole, and the Rock of Ages are examples. The biggest of these chambers (the Big Room) is 2,000 feet long and 200 feet from floor to soaring ceiling. The walls are hung with rock draperies. (The stalagmites grow from the floor up, the stalactites from the ceiling down.)

The full tour starts at the natural entrance to the cave and gives visitors a fine look at the caverns as the trail winds along the floor then high along a comfortingly wide ledge on one wall. Improbable as it may seem, a box luncheon is served at a restaurant located halfway along the trail, 750 feet below the surface. A shortened tour starts with the elevator ride down to the central area of the caverns, where it joins the other visitors for a stroll around the Big Room. Every tourist returns to the visitor center on the surface by elevator.

THE GIANT DOME DWARFS *its lesser neighbors and all who come to view it in the Big Room. The column rises 62 feet above the floor, its diameter approaches 20 feet.*

ANSEL ADAMS

The caverns are 56° the year around, whether the desert above is enduring the 0° winds of winter or the 100° heat of summer.

There is a surface side to the park, which supports a busy desert life community. Most of it is nocturnal, and the star attraction is the evening bat flight. The bat caves themselves are not open to touring; although bats are quite clean, their quarters are not. The best views of this striking spectacle are near the cavern mouth, where a ranger naturalist gives a short explanation of what is about to happen, just before the swirling storm erupts, within a few minutes of sundown. The greatest flights are in summer, when the whole colony is in residence and actively pursuing night-flying insects. A great number of the bats migrate south for the winter; in the coldest season the remaining ones go into a state of suspended animation, and the flights dwindle to nothing.

The park also has an abundance of small mammals, desert reptiles, and birds living in its scrub vegetation. Careful observation will reveal ground squirrels, skunks, raccoons, ringtails, foxes, many types of lizards, turkey vultures, and an occasional golden eagle.

The presence of the caverns has been known for a thousand years. Some wandering Indians used the cavern mouth for shelter but they did not test the temper of any god of the underworld by penetrating far inside. That was left to the turn-of-the-century bat guano miners. One of them, a young resident of the area, named James Larkin White, found himself drawn to serious explorations. His interest grew to passion, and his passion led to the establishment of the caverns as a national monument in 1923, and a national park in 1930. White's reward was a term as chief ranger of the park he helped establish.

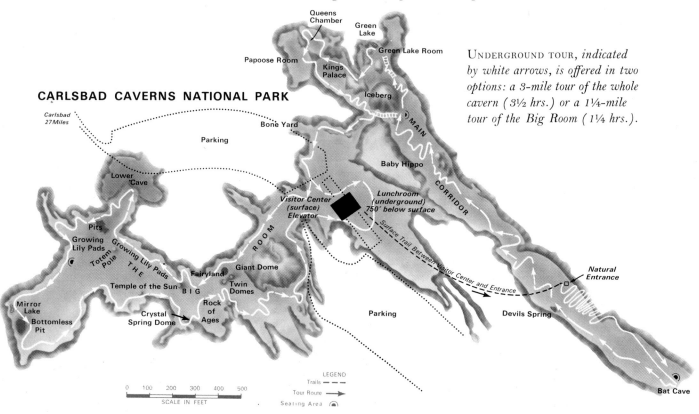

CARLSBAD CAVERNS NATIONAL PARK

UNDERGROUND TOUR, *indicated by white arrows, is offered in two options: a 3-mile tour of the whole cavern (3½ hrs.) or a 1¼-mile tour of the Big Room (1¼ hrs.).*

Queens Chamber
Green Lake
Green Lake Room
Papoose Room
Kings Palace
Iceberg
Carlsbad 27 Miles
Bone Yard
Parking
MAIN CORRIDOR
Baby Hippo
Lower Cave
Visitor Center (surface) Elevator
Lunchroom (underground) 750' below surface
Surface Trail Between Visitor Center and Entrance
Pits
Growing Lily Pads
Totem Pole
Growing Lily Pads
THE BIG ROOM
Fairyland
Giant Dome
Temple of the Sun
Twin Domes
Natural Entrance
Mirror Lake
Crystal Spring Dome
Rock of Ages
Bottomless Pit
Parking
Devils Spring
Bat Cave

LEGEND
Trails — — —
Tour Route ⟶
Seating Area

0 100 200 300 400 500
SCALE IN FEET

EACH DROP OF WATER *passing through the caverns deposits minute cargo of mineral. Where drops come slowly, a needle stalactite forms. Where they come faster, a column may form connecting ceiling to floor.*

HOW THE CAVERNS WERE FORMED

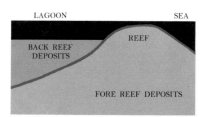

200 MILLION YEARS AGO

LAGOON   SEA

BACK REEF DEPOSITS   REEF

FORE REEF DEPOSITS

ABOUT 200 MILLION YEARS AGO, *dome of the cavern formation was a reef in a Permian sea. The sea deposited sediments in the lagoon, then rose and covered whole reef with deep deposits. Two succeeding uplifts of the earth's crust (which formed the Rocky Mountains then the Guadalupes) raised the formation above water table. Fractures in the limestone allowed seepage that formed the caverns, then seepage of ground water from rain and snow fashioned rock sculptures.*

WATER LEVEL

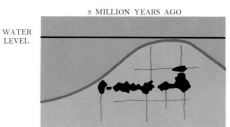

3 MILLION YEARS AGO

1 MILLION YEARS AGO

RECENT

VISITOR CENTER

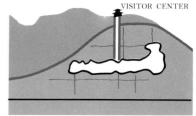

IN THE DOLL'S THEATER *the curtain is a gossamer web of stalactites. These crystalline limestone forms are incredibly brittle, breaking at a touch.*

THE BEAUTIFUL HUES *can be explained in scientific terms. The rock is calcite or aragonite—crystalline forms of limestone—colored by iron oxide or other minerals in the same way as is the Petrified Forest or Bryce Canyon. But their rich luster when they are wet defies chemical analysis and awes all who come to see them.*

CARLSBAD CAVERNS   **195**

MEXICAN FREE-TAILED BAT

THE REMARKABLE SONAR OF BATS

A BAT CAN NAB A MOSQUITO *on the wing, dodge a wind-whipped tree limb, and wing merrily on his way through the blackest night of the year. How? The bats that live in these caves are in effect FM transmitters. They emit a high-frequency note which exceeds by many times the range of a human voice, yet lasts a thousandth of a second or less. They hear the minute portion of their sound that is reflected by prey—or an obstacle—and "lock in" with ever-faster beeps until they nab the food or dodge the obstacle with a daring bit of aerobatics. Scientists find it very difficult to jam the emissions, but impaired hearing or muting renders a bat nearly helpless in flight.*

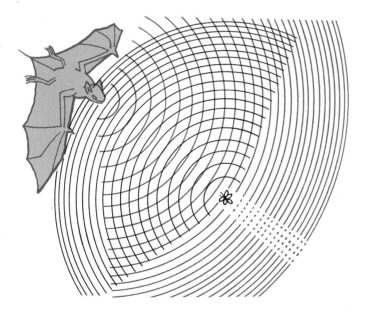

COUNTLESS THOUSANDS OF BATS FLY OUT *of their cavern in the span of half an hour, starting right at sundown. In-flight collision is extremely rare. They fan out over a 50-mile radius to catch and eat several tons of winged insects before dawn, then return to sleep the day away, hanging head down in dense clusters. Fourteen species share the space. The Mexican free-tailed bat is commonest. Others: fringed myotis, western pipistrel, lump-nosed, and pallid.*

CARLSBAD CAVERNS **197**

ROCKY MOUNTAIN

ASTRIDE THE CONTINENTAL DIVIDE

PARK FACTS: *Location:* North central Colorado. *Discovered:* 1859. *Established:* January 26, 1915. *Size:* 410 sq. mi. *Altitude:* 7,620 to 14,256 feet. *Climate:* Cool, pleasant; perpetual snows mantle highest summits and valley walls. *Season:* All year, but main cross-park highway, Trail Ridge Road, closed in winter. *Visitors in 1968:* 2,187,573.

THIS IS THE HIGH COUNTRY. The skyline is saw-toothed with jutting granite, unsoftened by vegetation, for timberline is at 11,500 feet. From one spot you can count 72 peaks that rise above that height. Eighteen to more than 13,000 feet. Snow patches remain on the crags year-round in protected spots, and high cirques preserve the remnants of glaciers.

Rocky Mountain National Park has been called a primer of glacial geology. Even the most casual observer must notice the great rock amphitheaters where the glaciers formed, the U-shaped valleys carved when the ice began to move, the moraines where the loose rocks collected. Only a few small glaciers are found here now, but the marks left by ice are all around.

Guardian of all is lofty Longs Peak, whose summit rises to 14,256 feet. It dominates the range and can be seen from far out on the plains to the east.

The park takes in about 410 square miles of the most scenic part of north-central Colorado. Below the towering peaks is a high vacationland of quiet lakes and plunging streams, grassy meadows and rugged gorges. Thick forests shelter countless wild creatures.

One of the remarkable aspects of the park is its widespread alpine tundra, that dense carpet of miniature plants that thrives in cold climate. Another is the large number of bighorn sheep, among the rarest of wild animals in North America. You may also see golden eagles, industrious beavers, herds of elk.

Despite the rugged terrain, the park is easily accessible. Much of its splendor can be viewed at a distance from main roads. The most famous, Trail Ridge Road, reaches an altitude of 12,183 feet and stays above timberline for 11 miles.

THUNDER LAKE, NESTLED IN A GLACIAL BASIN, *is one of the scores of lakes and ponds scattered throughout the park, mostly accessible only by trail. Many of the smaller lakelets are beaver-engineered.*

DAVID MUENCH

To enjoy this park to the fullest, to experience both its grandeur and its quiet peace, you must penetrate it by trail. Such exquisite spots as Loch Vale, Jewel, Fern, and Odessa lakes are reached only by those willing to walk or ride on horseback. More than 300 miles of trails lead to such rewarding destinations.

The park is open all year. Spring is shy and waits until late April or early May to display its finery. The long days of summer, when the sun is warm and the lakes and sky rich blue, are followed by the spectacular advent of the Colorado autumn. The mountain foliage blazes scarlet and gold, the days grow crisp, and through the clear air you may hear the trumpeted challenge of the big bull elk as he gathers his harem. Then the snows come again, a white blanket settles over the Rockies, and the skiers and snowshoers come back into their own.

Those who today enjoy the bounties of this mountain playground can thank one man for preserving it for their pleasure. Enos Mills, writer and naturalist, sometimes called the "John Muir of the Rockies," campaigned for the park for years against strong opposition. When at length it was established in 1915, its creation was universally credited to the persistence of Mills and his followers.

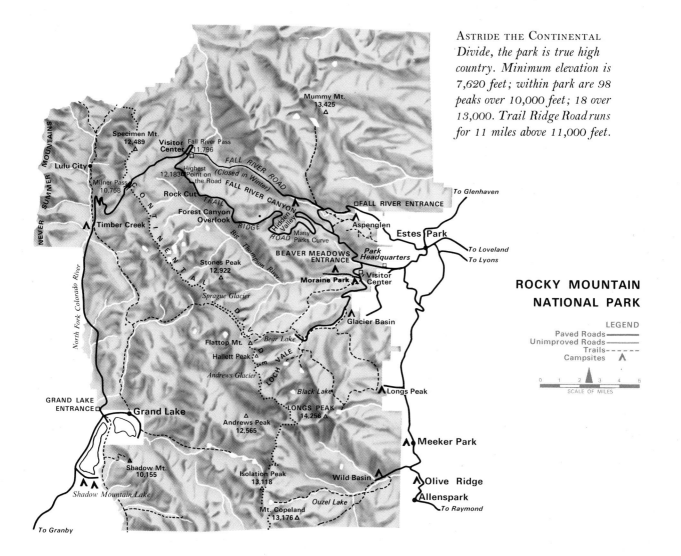

ASTRIDE THE CONTINENTAL *Divide, the park is true high country. Minimum elevation is 7,620 feet; within park are 98 peaks over 10,000 feet; 18 over 13,000. Trail Ridge Road runs for 11 miles above 11,000 feet.*

ROCKY MOUNTAIN NATIONAL PARK

LEGEND
Paved Roads
Unimproved Roads
Trails
Campsites

GLACIAL ODDITY, *a chunk of hard rock stands poised on a pedestal of softer stone that was almost worn away by erosion. Rockies in this area are composed of a mixture of hard granites and gneisses.*

THE QUEST FOR BEAVER *by fur trappers opened much of the Rocky Mountain area to exploration in the early 1800's. Beavers are still active within the park, where they dam quiet streams and lake margins, fell willow and aspen saplings for food, and build snug shelters.*

ROCKY MOUNTAIN   **201**

DEBONAIR, PIPE-SMOKING MOUNTAINEER *gets ready to rappel down from an ascent of Eagle Cliff. By paying out rope, he will lower himself gently to the ground below. Rope is run through a loop secured to piton driven into the rock; it permits quick and safe descent after the laborious climb. In distance: Longs Peak.*

NEARLY EXTINGUISHED BY HUNTERS *before the park was established, the elk (wapiti) are a common sight now. Importation of elk from Yellowstone helped restore the herd.*

"ABOVE TIMBERLINE" *is a phrase that takes on real meaning in Rocky Mountain National Park. At Rock Cut, nearly 12,000-foot elevation and almost 600 feet above the tree line, densely-wooded Forest Canyon is far below.*

GLACIER

THE INTERNATIONAL PARK

PARK FACTS: *Location:* Northwestern Montana. *Discovered:* 1800's. *Established:* Nat. park, May 11, 1910; made part of Waterton-Glacier International Peace Park, May 22, 1932. *Size:* 1,600 sq. mi. *Altitude:* 3,154-10,448 ft. *Climate:* Summers warm days, chilly nights. *Season:* All year, but passes closed Oct.-May. *Visitors, 1969:* 1,032,272 (10 months).

THE MOUNTAINS OF GLACIER ARE NOT HIGH, compared with those in some national parks, but there is something distinctive about their sheer faces and angular contours that led the early French explorer Pierre Verendrye to call this "the land of shining mountains." There is something hospitable about them, too; their flanks are covered by heavy forests that descend to the edge of sapphire lakes and seem to welcome visitors. Above timberline their upper reaches are multicolored—blue-grey, buff, green, red, purple.

Straddling the Continental Divide in northwest Montana, Glacier contains an accessible but unspoiled wilderness penetrated by a thousand miles of trails. Here you can travel alone for an hour or a week, or you can take a guided trip without charge. There are saddle horses for those who want to rent them, and shelter cabins for those who reach the remote back country.

It is a land of colorful place names: Gunsight and Two Medicine are mountain passes, and Rising Wolf, Scalplock, and Going-to-the-Sun are mountains. And there are Indian names like Kintla and Appekunny, for this is Blackfoot country. The eastern part of the park was reservation until the Blackfeet sold it in 1896. They are still in evidence, for their present home adjoins the park on the east.

This is a park that deserves ample time—time to meditate and relax, to hike and ride, to study and observe, to fish and camp. John Muir was emphatic: "Give a month at least to this precious reserve. The time will not be taken from the sum of your life. Instead of shortening, it will indefinitely lengthen it and make you truly immortal."

Glacier's northernmost boundary is on the 49th parallel, and even though its mountains reach a height of only 10,448 feet, the northern latitude means

SPECTACULAR GOING-TO-THE-SUN ROAD *crosses The Continental Divide at Logan Pass (6,664 ft.) within sight of pyramidal Reynolds Mountain (9,167 ft.). The Mayan-temple shape of this peak is typical of mountains in park, which were carved by glaciers from soft, layered rock.*

205

WATERTON-GLACIER INTERNATIONAL
Peace Park is only park in world to cross an international boundary, include land in two countries. Park straddles Continental Divide. Only one road crosses park, but railroad and accompanying road skirt the southern edge. Spur roads lead in to the major lake resorts.

LEGEND
Paved Roads ————
Unimproved Roads ————
Trails - - - - - -
Campsites ∧
National Boundaries —— ··· ——

GLACIER NATIONAL PARK

abundant snow. The snowfall and dozens of glaciers within the park feed more than 200 lakes and rushing streams. Water seems to be everywhere, in lush verdant valleys, in meadows ablaze with wildflowers, along roads, and nestling in glacial cirques at the base of sheer rock walls. Water is so abundant that the visitor is seldom out of sight of a lake or out of hearing of a waterfall or stream.

Although this is a trail park of the first magnitude, the roads are excellent and the scenic Going-to-the-Sun Road is one of the most spectacular in America. The roads within the park are not generally passable much before June 15, but if weather permits they are kept open until mid-October.

Adjoining Glacier on the north is Canada's Waterton Lakes National Park, and together they form the Waterton-Glacier International Peace Park, dedicated in 1932 to the permanent peace and friendship of the two neighboring nations. By all means, cross the boundary for a visit to the Canadian park. There are no border complications, and the boat trips, fine food, and English shops will remain in your memory as a pleasant adjunct to your Glacier trip.

FROM THE 10,033 FOOT SUMMIT *of Mount Jackson (left),* *an extensive sea of peaks is visible for a hundred miles in* *all directions. The peak stands on the Continental Divide.* *Rain falling on the western slopes of the Divide eventually* *runs into the Pacific Ocean; that falling on the eastern* *side runs off into Hudson Bay.*

BE-WHISKERED MOUNTAIN GOAT, *native to this craggy* *domain, may be encountered near trails or resorts. Tolerant* *of tourists, goats often come within camera range. These* *nimble animals rely on their agility to elude predators* *that seek them out in their rocky lairs. Profile of this park* *native decorates the boxcars of the Great Northern.*

GLACIER   207

GLACIER EXPLORING, HORSEBACK
*riding, fishing are some of the attractions
that make the Many Glacier area popular.
(ABOVE) Rock-strewn surface of
Grinnell Glacier lies just ahead of hikers,
7 miles out of Many Glacier. Stones fall
from cliffs behind, are gradually carried
to melting snout. Note crevasses along
edge. (BELOW) Assembly of saddle horses
awaits riders at Many Glacier Hotel.
Chalet-style architecture typical of
resorts throughout park.*

CLEAR, COLD WATER OF JOSEPHINE LAKE *reflects the
bulky form of Mount Gould (9,551 ft.). Size of the
mountains is easy to gauge because the wide
horizontal bands and strong lines of vertical joints give
scale that viewer can relate to scene close by, far away.*

HALF IN CANADA, HALF IN THE UNITED STATES, *Waterton Lake occupies a long glacial trench between towering crags. At the Canadian end, town of Waterton offers shopping and resort facilities, crowned by the striking Prince of Wales Hotel* (ABOVE), *perched on a promontory with a commanding view of the lake. Waterton is accessible by trail, launch, sightseeing bus, or family car. The motor launch* International (ABOVE RIGHT) *runs from Waterton to the U.S. Ranger Station in Montana, stops along the way to pick up hikers, let passengers explore. Here, boat is docked opposite Olson Creek, 3 miles inside Montana. Launches also run on all the major resort lakes.*

SHOWIEST OF THE PARK'S WILDFLOWERS, *beargrass is often considered the park's flower. Member of the lily family, it starts blooming in June in valleys, continues into August in high country. Like other alpine parks, Glacier puts on an extraordinary display of color after snows melt.*

RAY ATKESON

MARTIN LITTON

FROM A VISTA POINT *on the Going-to-the-Sun Highway, the motorist can look down the valley of the McDonald River far below. The road descends to the river and follows it to resort-lined Lake McDonald.*

PEAKS OF GARDEN WALL *rise in brooding majesty along spine of the Continental Divide. Sweeping view, encompassing acres of glacier lilies, looks north from Logan Pass.*

YELLOWSTONE

THE GRAND OLD PARK

PARK FACTS: *Location:* Northwestern Wyoming. *Discovered:* 1807. *Established:* Mar. 1, 1872. *Size:* 3,472 sq. mi. *Altitude:* 5,314 to 11,360 ft. *Climate:* Mild summer days, cool nights, rain in June. Winter temperatures from below freezing; heavy snowfall. *Season:* All year (official season May 1-Oct. 31). *Visitors in 1968: 2,229,657.*

YELLOWSTONE IS THE "TYPICAL" NATIONAL PARK of anecdote and caricature, of plentiful over-friendly bears, of elbow-to-elbow fishermen and hopelessly tangled trout lines, and of incredible summer hordes of wandering tourists.

On the other side of the coin, Yellowstone works a magic spell in return for nothing but time and attention. It is not a place that jibes with personal time-tables. Travelers go to Yellowstone to witness things happening more than to look at static scenery, and seldom—at any site—will nature's performance coincide with one's arrival. So the visitor moves along, trusting to luck, or settles down and waits. In good time, sunlight reaches the bottom of a golden canyon and a waterfall's spray rises through rainbows. An osprey finally alights on the pinnacle-top nest in the telephoto viewfinder. The bull moose emerges from forest shadow and wades out into a marsh. A family of playful young grizzlies comes wrestling and tumbling through a wind-rippled prairie. A brown trout—big enough to feed a whole family—takes the lure and then sounds. The Sapphire Pool belches a brief alert and then explodes into snowy jets that climb for the sky.

There is hot-spring activity of one kind or another in many countries. But nowhere is there so much of it, nowhere is it so spectacular, and nowhere has it been so considerately cared for.

Neither color illustrations nor postcards can memorialize the diverse beauty of the countless ways hot water comes out of the ground in Yellowstone: the flooding colors of spectrum and algae, the transparence of bubble-starred pools dropping away into darkness, the echoed thumping of unheralded distant geysers in the night, the smell of hydrogen sulfide, the sky-flung plumes of water.

THE AWESOME GORGE OF THE YELLOWSTONE RIVER *is a stunning surprise to travelers when they first encounter it. The gentle, forested countryside scarcely prepares the visitor for such a spectacular sight. The chasm walls glow with reds, ochres, and yellows (the park takes its name from this colorful canyon).*

215

ANSEL ADAMS

So unbelievable were the tales about Yellowstone *told by the first explorers that two expeditions were sent to the region to determine the truth, if any, in their reports. This photograph, taken in 1871 by photographer W. H. Jackson, shows the second fact-finding expedition, the Geological Survey's Hayden Expedition. Reports of this party plus Jackson's photographs helped convince Congress that Yellowstone country should be made a national park.*

Although the wonders of Yellowstone were discovered in 1807 and rumors about them circulated for decades, they were laughed off as tall tales, too fantastic to believe, until nearly 1870.

Actual discovery is credited to a member of the Lewis and Clark expedition named John Colter, who left the group to explore and trap on his own. By 1837, the story of his adventures was widely enough known to have reached novelist Washington Irving who noted that Colter had given such an account of Yellowstone's "gloomy terrors, its hidden fires, smoking pits, noxious streams, and the all-pervading 'smell of brimstone,' that it received, and has ever since retained among trappers the name of 'Colter's Hell'."

Trappers wandered throughout Yellowstone for 60 years after Colter's visit, and tales about its marvels were common among them. However, little of the information reached the general public. The mountain men were a close-knit and unlettered fraternity, and they were known as braggarts and liars, and their stories were accepted as typical frontier "roarbacks."

But as settlement advanced in the territories nearby, prominent citizens began to take an interest in checking into these preposterous tales. In 1869, a party of three men spent more than a month exploring the eastern geyser basins and reported their findings to a still skeptical public. Their observations, however, spurred a more famous group to follow the trail to Yellowstone. This was the Washburn-Langford-Doane expedition, whose exploits led to the founding of the national park system, as described in the opening chapter.

This party of nineteen men, full of exuberance and wonder, systematically explored the area, keeping careful records as they progressed. They named the thermal features—favoring the Devil and all his works—but by common agreement, they refrained from naming anything for themselves. (Their names were later bestowed on some of the peaks and rivers.) After completing their survey, they met at a famous campfire at the intersection of the Gibbon, Firehole, and Madison rivers and there reached the historic decision to work for legislation to protect the wonderland from exploitation.

After returning home, they lectured, published articles in magazines and newspapers, and campaigned to have the area set aside as a public preserve. As an early result of their pressures, United States Geologist F. V. Hayden led a scientific expedition to Yellowstone to authenticate their findings. His enthusiastic endorsement of their observations, coupled with a superb set of photographs by W. H. Jackson, helped to speed the enactment of the historic legislation that created the first national park in the world in 1872.

FROM FREEMAN TILDEN'S "FOLLOWING THE FRONTIER"

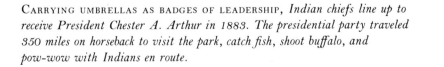

CARRYING UMBRELLAS AS BADGES OF LEADERSHIP, *Indian chiefs line up to receive President Chester A. Arthur in 1883. The presidential party traveled 350 miles on horseback to visit the park, catch fish, shoot buffalo, and pow-wow with Indians en route.*

PERCHED ON THE BRITTLE FORMATIONS *of Minerva Terrace,*
a touring party of women and children strike a formal
pose for photographer Frank J. Haynes in 1888.

Unfortunately, far-sighted as the legislators were for their day, they did not provide for all eventualities in the new law nor did they appropriate funds, and the park administration struggled for years sorely handicapped.

The park was located miles from nowhere and in the midst of territory still plagued by unfriendly Indians. Just four years after creation of the park, General Custer suffered his last stand a scant 130 miles away. In 1877, the Nez Perce in the closing days of their bloody 1,600-mile retreat from Oregon, captured a party of tourists camped on Firehole River and killed two from another party. A few days later, the warriors were defeated in their final battle north of the park. When, two years later, the park superintendent's headquarters was erected, it was equipped with a gun turret on the roof.

Even after the Indians were quieted, tourists faced an arduous trek to reach the park. In 1878, they had a choice of two routes: a northern one from Bismarck that was 1,052 miles long—820 miles by steamboat and 232 by stagecoach—and took 12 to 14 days. The southern access from Ogden required 1,183 miles of train travel followed by 472 miles of stagecoaching, a combination that consumed 10 days.

Even after the tourists began to flow into the park, there were sticky problems in abundance. Not enough rangers were on hand to protect the geysers from vandalism, politicians gave away lucrative concessions to friends, and the "protected" game was so wantonly slaughtered, even by early park officials, that some species were nearly extinguished, most notably the buffalo. In 1883 administration was turned over to the Army, which built roads and ran the park with quiet efficiency until 1916, when the Park System took over. Since then, affairs of this vast, complex, and over-popular park have been carried on by the Park Service and its concessioners with consummate skill.

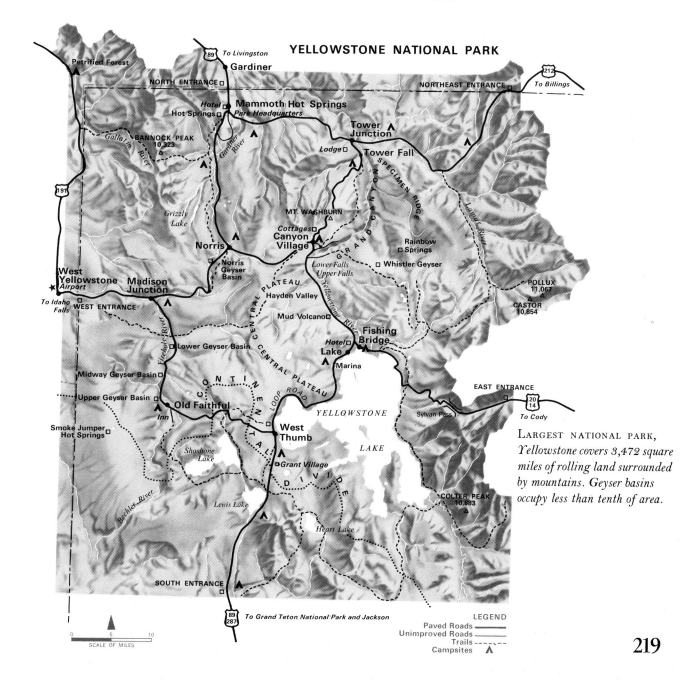

LARGEST NATIONAL PARK, *Yellowstone covers 3,472 square miles of rolling land surrounded by mountains. Geyser basins occupy less than tenth of area.*

219

Thermal Areas

THE EARTH'S INNER HEAT, close to the surface of the ground all the way across the wide plateau, is the why and wherefore of Yellowstone's renown. In many parts of the park, the ground is warm or hot to the touch, and while this heating is accomplished by heated water or gases coming up through the crust, there is every likelihood that the temperature of the rock itself reaches the melting point less than a mile below the surface. Ground water moves easily into and through the porous, fissured surface rocks, eventually working its way down to depths where temperatures far exceed the boiling point, and forming reservoirs of super-heated steam. Under extreme pressure, the steam seeks a way out. It may reach the atmosphere again as a steady roaring jet that becomes visible only as it condenses to vapor some distance above the ground; then it is a steam vent, or fumarole. Or it may have its exit clogged by inflowing liquid water, which it must push out of the way; then it becomes a geyser.

A typical geyser eruption may begin with a flow, or an increase in flow, of water from the orifice, accompanied by deep-seated cannonading that seems to shake the ground and indicates that the restraining pressure is off. Then the column of water in the tube is thrown upward for a few seconds, or a few minutes, by steam that continues to rumble underground and roar skyward for some time after the water is expelled. The force of the steam jet dies down as the sub-terranean pressure is relieved, and water again begins to fill the exhaust tube, blocking the exit of the steam and setting the stage for the next eruption.

SNOWMOBILERS GATHER *at Old Faithful, which puts on its most spectacular show in freezing weather. Touring groups of snowmobilers drive in from outside the park or from Mammoth Hot Springs.*

As it has for three centuries, *Old Faithful sends its towering plume of 12,000 gallons of boiling water into the thin mountain air. Famous the world over, the great geyser has attracted travelers to Yellowstone since 1870, when its existence was first reported to a disbelieving public. With reasonable faithfulness, the geyser erupts every 33 to 96 minutes for 4 or 5 minutes and then subsides. Its display is most spectacular in cool weather or early morning when the superheated water meets cold air and condenses into billowing steam.*

MARTIN LITTON

ENDLESS VARIETY CHARACTERIZES THE EXPULSION *of hot water and steam from the heated depths of the earth in the geyser basins. Where heated water is free to move to the surface, it bubbles out in hot springs. At Grand Prismatic Spring (Midway Basin), a gentle, pulsing flow covers a large area with a shallow, terraced pond. Where steam finds an easy passage to the surface, it comes out as a steam vent, or fumarole, such as the marshmallow-like formation (ABOVE RIGHT) in the Firehole Lake area that gives off wisps of steam to the accompaniment of guttural boilings and thumpings.*

A GEYSER'S UNDERGROUND PLUMBING SYSTEM

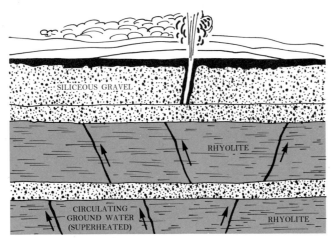

SILICEOUS GRAVEL

RHYOLITE

CIRCULATING
GROUND WATER
(SUPERHEATED)

RHYOLITE

WHAT GOES ON INSIDE A GEYSER? *Water seeps down through porous volcanic soil and collects in chambers where it is turned to steam by superheated earth. The chambers all connect with a central vent which fills with water. Weight of the water in the main tube blocks escape of steam from the chambers. In time, steam is superheated to a point where it explosively expels the water in the tube into the air.*

EARLY IN THE MORNING *in Norris Geyser Basin, steam condenses in the cold air to form a forest of white, drifting plumes. A boardwalk safely conducts visitors through the active area. Twenty-seven geysers are located here, most of them minor performers that erupt only a few feet. Stars of the basin: Ledge Geyser, which rises 125 feet once a day, and the constantly erupting Steamboat Geyser that sometimes shoots up from its normal 20-30 feet to 380 feet.*

224 YELLOWSTONE

HOT WATER SEEPING OUT A MOUNTAINSIDE *in the Mammoth Hot Springs area evaporates to leave level terraces of travertine. As the terrace edges grow upward, water may break through and flow down and outward to form new terraces, leaving old ones high and dry. Algae colors pools and terrace edges. In background: Mammoth, with hotel in center and former Fort Yellowstone (park headquarters) on right.*

NORTH OF OLD FAITHFUL *is a series of geyser basins and thermal wonders close to the road to Mammoth. Castle Geyser* (ABOVE), *so-named because of its fancied resemblance to the ruins of an old castle tower, spouts 65 to 100 feet every 8 to 10 hours. It is located in Upper Geyser Basin.*

STEAM RISES CONSTANTLY *from Fountain Geyser Pool* (RIGHT ABOVE), *one of a cluster of geysers and hot springs presumably connected by a common underground water system in Lower Geyser Basin. From the side of Roaring Mountain* (RIGHT), *steam rises from hundreds of vents. The mountain is named for a single vent that gave forth a loud roar for months in 1902 during a period of intense activity. After the opening became enlarged, the noise quieted down and the mountain now gives off its steam in relative quiet.*

YELLOWSTONE **227**

Back Country

HORSES AND HIKERS CAN GO over Yellowstone's gentle grades at speeds unheard of in the Sierra Nevada, Cascades, or Coast Ranges. The woods, waters, and wide open spaces beckon, yet the back-country trails are just beginning to be used. In the past, little or no information or encouragement was offered to facilitate wilderness trail travel, and there are still no facilities within the park for equipping parties for overnight rides or hiking trips. But this is changing rapidly. Guided horseback rides of short duration are available at several locations and the concessioner offers week-long guided pack trips into the Gallatin Canyon area.

Most of the travel into the primitive corners of Yellowstone comes from outside the boundaries. Pack trips originating at dude ranches and pack stations around the perimeter often loop into the park, taking admirable advantage of its fine high country and productive fishing. Cooke City, 4 miles outside the Northeast Entrance, is a favorite jumping-off point for the high and rugged Absaroka Range along the east side of the park.

MARTIN LITTON

ONE OF THE ORIGINAL STAGECOACHES *that brought tourists into the park until 1917 heads for an evening cook-out in a quiet valley near Tower Junction. Here and there, wide-sweeping meadows push back the lodgepole forest and create spring wildflower parks and grazing land for antelope, deer, bison, and moose.*

BASALT COLUMNS FORM A BANDOLEER PATTERN *along the edge of the cliffs*
near Tower Junction. The dark band is in sharp contrast to the colorful,
deeply eroded canyon wall. The basalt was deposited as a lava overflow in
the dim geologic past on top of sandstones built up under an inland sea.

YELLOWSTONE **229**

RIVERS MEANDER BETWEEN GRASSY *banks in the park-like valleys of Yellowstone. The Firehole River snakes through a half dozen geyser basins. In some sections, its riverbed is warmed by hot springs. (Oldtimers claimed the bed was heated by fast-running water.)*

THE SMELL OF BACON *and coffee rises from a camp in the Gallatin Mountains, an over-night stop for concessioner-operated saddle trips into the back country.*

THE PACKTRAIN PLODDING THROUGH THE WILDFLOWERS *is on its way to Cascade Corner, the mountainous southwest section of the park, noted for waterfalls, cascades, and fishing streams. An extensive trail system, originally developed by the Army for supply routes, leads to a magnificent, uncrowded backcountry.*

A WATER WORLD FOR CANOERS *is an exclusive feature of Yellowstone National Park. Three arms of huge Yellowstone Lake and nearby Lake Shoshone are reserved for paddlers only. As these protected waters are game refuges, oarsmen can expect to see waterfowl, moose, and an occasional grizzly at the water's edge.*

LONGER THAN ITS CARRIER, *a 3-passenger canoe is trussed down for the ride to the lake country.*

The Animals

THERE IS TRUTH IN THE SAYING THAT Yellowstone National Park is the greatest wildlife sanctuary in the United States, but that is not so much a statement of abundance of wildlife in Yellowstone as of poverty elsewhere. Of large native animals summering on the park's 3,472 square miles, only one species—the American elk or wapiti—is numbered in the thousands (the count has been fluctuating between 10,000 and 15,000 in recent years). The populations of black bear, moose, and pronghorn seldom if ever exceed 500 each; there may be nearly a thousand mule deer at times, but figures of 200 or so are probably tops for grizzly and bighorn. Yellowstone's "concentration" of bison amounts to an average of about one animal to 3½ square miles—proving that the thundering herd is indeed a thing of the past.

Beyond the range of the automobile, encounters with wildlife will be full of magic. If you recognize the deep, rolling call, you will pause to stalk a sandhill crane. If you see swans in the park in summer, you will know they are rare trumpeters; whistlers are spring and fall migrants only. If you have learned to handle a paddle efficiently and silently, the otter may let you come almost abreast of him before he dives. If you know how to stand or sit perfectly still, the curious antelope may move toward you instead of away from you. Small animals and birds are very much the same as in other mountain regions of the West.

JOSEPH VAN WORMER

FAWN, WITH SNOW ON ITS MUZZLE FROM *winter grazing, is member of the numerous clan of mule deer, beloved by the touring public for their grace and shy persistence around humans. Deer are most likely to be seen at Mammoth Hot Springs, Indian Creek, Chittenden Bridge, and West Thumb. Unlike its over-abundant cousins, the elk, the deer population within the park keeps in balance with its food supply.*

ELK PLOW THROUGH DEEP SNOW *on the winter range in search of food. The bulk of the 13,000-animal herd spends summer in the mountains and then crowds into the lowlands in winter in desperate competition for the available food. Grass is gone or covered with deep snow, trees are bare of leaves, and there is not enough food to keep all the elk alive. Hundreds die each winter, but the herd continues to grow because of absence of cougars and wolves that would keep it in balance.*

IN FEW PLACES IN THE UNITED STATES *can antelope be seen in their natural state. A herd of 350 ranges over the plains near Mammoth Hot Springs. Sharp-eyed and nervous, they are easily spooked, and if alarmed, they sweep over the fields in swift and graceful flight. Pronghorns of both sexes are armed with sharp, hollow horns that they shed each year.*

YELLOWSTONE **235**

BELLIGERENT COUSINS OF FAMILIAR BLACK *bear , grizzlies keep to themselves in wild areas; distinguished by shoulder hump, great size.*

SENT UPSTAIRS FOR SAFETY, *cubs are taught to climb for self-protection. Black bears can "swim" up trees with ease; often perch on limbs.*

JUDICIAL-LOOKING BEAR *surveys the passing scene along the highway. The unconsciously comical poses that bears assume endear them to tourists but cause the poor beasts to receive more attention than they should for their own good.*

JOSEPH VAN WORMER

PEYTON MONCURE

CUBS STAY CLOSE TO MOTHER *for as long as a year. No bigger than a squirrel when born in early spring, they are capable of caring for themselves after a year of intensive training by the mother.*

PANHANDLING BEARS *set up shop along the main highways, take the same stations day after day to wheedle tidbits from soft-hearted tourists. Human food is unhealthful for them and dulls their appetite for natural fare. Although generally shy around people, they sometimes turn aggressive, particularly by fall when they have accumulated a summer's indignities and frustrations from dealing with the public. Dangerous when crossed or teased, they can move as swiftly as a cat.*

RAY ATKESON   BISON GRAZE IN GEYSER BASINS *in winter because warmth keeps snow melted and exposes the grass. Natural salt licks around mineral springs provide an essential part of their diet. Although a plains animal, bison have readily adapted to the park environment ever since the initial herd was augmented with 21 animals purchased by Congress in 1902. There are now 400 in the park herd. Bison had nearly been exterminated in the 1880's by ruthless hunting, despite protective laws passed in 1864.*

COW AND CALF IN LATE SNOW. *Cows usually give birth to one calf a year, which is born in late spring. Calves accompany their mothers to the mountains a month or two after they are born.*

AGE-LONG PARTNERS IN PLAINS LIVING, *bull and bird examine each other with respectful curiosity.*

GRAND TETON

RENDEZVOUS FOR MOUNTAINEERS

PARK FACTS: *Location:* West central Wyoming. *Discovered:* 1807. *Established:* February 26, 1929; Jackson Hole added September 14, 1950. *Size:* 485 sq. mi. *Altitude:* 6,400-13,770 feet. *Climate:* Warm, dry summers with cool nights, occasional storms. Winter snows average 120 inches. *Season:* All year. *Visitors in 1968:* 2,970,255.

THE TETONS RISE FROM THE COUNTRYSIDE around them like a craggy island from the sea. Few American landscapes are more dramatic, more awe-inspiring, or more beautiful than these mountains of northwest Wyoming. From 100 or even 50 miles away, they seem little more than wisps of cloud. As you draw closer they begin to assume more substantial form, then suddenly their full impact strikes you, as if they had exploded from the level floor of Jackson Hole. Many ranges are more extensive and many mountains are higher, gradually ascending with foothills as stepping-stones. But there is nothing gradual about the Tetons in their sheer, 7,000-foot rise from the level plain.

Grand Teton National Park contains a little less than 500 square miles. It is smaller than many, but within it is packed more scenery, more history, more animals, more boating and fishing, more hiking and mountain climbing, more opportunity for enjoyment and relaxation than in many areas twice its size.

The scenic grandeur of the Tetons is that of the Sierra Nevada or of the Rockies telescoped into a range less than 40 miles long. The majesty of the Grand Teton, with its 13,770-foot summit and its companion peaks, Mount Owen, and South and Middle Tetons, reflected in the placid waters of Jenny Lake, is almost overwhelming. Glaciers nestle in the cirques, streams tumble and cascade from high places, mountain lakes reflect the blue of a Wyoming sky, and in the valley below, the Snake River winds its way to Jackson Lake and on eventually to the Columbia.

Two hundred miles of trails beckon the hiker and horseman—trails that lead to lakes buried in virgin wilderness, through deep canyons, over high passes above timberline, and to mountaintops. There are trails for every mood and

ALWAYS IN VIEW FROM NEARLY EVERY PART OF THE PARK, *jagged Teton Range catches and holds the eye. "Mountains without foothills," the peaks rise straight from the valley. Here, viewed from a mountain trail, is Cathedral Group.*

241

every temperament, from short, level walks to long, strenuous hikes. The Tetons have long been the objective of serious climbers from this country and Europe—and few American peaks are more respected. Those who know are reluctant to rank the Alps above the Tetons in difficulty of ascent. It is little wonder that the last two peaks in this range were not conquered until 1930. Such climbs are not for the novice; for those who respond to the challenge, a mountaineering school operates here.

The history of the area has a fascination all its own. Probably the first white man to penetrate it was John Colter of the Lewis and Clark expedition in 1807. He was followed by the Astorians, who crossed Teton Pass in 1811. French-Canadian trappers in 1819 saw the three peaks from the west and referred to them as *Les Trois Tetons* (The Three Breasts).

From 1824 on, the area was a center of fur trade activity. Mountain men, among them Jim Bridger, William Sublette, Thomas Fitzpatrick, Jedediah Smith, Joseph Meek, knew the country well. One of the largest of the fur rendezvous, that of 1832, was held in Pierre's Hole across the range to the west. Still later in the 80's, it was cattle country; the town of Jackson yet retains a certain flavor of the days before tourists replaced steers in importance. Fictional characters, too, have furthered Jackson's fame. Here it was that the Virginian said, "When you call me that, *smile*," and it was to Honeymoon Island on Leigh Lake that he brought his bride. Owen Wister's book did much to publicize the romance of the Tetons.

As early as 1920, Jackson Hole was becoming known for its versions of the dude ranch, an institution that has grown in popularity over the years. Through it many an Easterner has fallen in love with the freedom and informality of Western life. It is here, for the first time, that many a tenderfoot has used a Western saddle and worn Western clothes; experienced the odors of sagebrush flats, pine forests, and a campfire; found luxury in falling asleep under the stars, and pleasure in the wash of windlashed rain in his face during a mountain storm.

Jackson Hole contains one of the largest remaining elk herds. Herds of 7,000 to 9,000 wintering on the National Elk Refuge north of Jackson, adjacent to the park, are a major attraction. Only a small exhibition herd remains behind when the elk moves to surrounding high country in the summer.

No road penetrates the mountainous west side of this park, but on the east, good highways traverse it in a general north-south direction. One skirts the east shore of Jackson and Jenny lakes at the very foot of the peaks reflected in their mirrors. The Jackson Hole Highway, a few miles to the east, follows the Snake River and affords a better opportunity to view the range as a whole.

Excellent campgrounds and picnic areas, as well as boat ramps, are strategically placed, and lodges and guest ranches are numerous.

The season of greatest activity is from early June through Labor Day, although the highway from Jackson through the park and over Togwotee Pass to the east is kept open throughout the winter. The park is approached from all four directions by highway.

THE MAGIC OF THE GRAND TETONS *has enthralled men ever since the*
range was first discovered. Indians, fur-traders, cattlemen, and tourists
have in succession felt the spell of this dramatic country. The symmetrical
mountains take on varying coloration, ranging from grey to blue to purple,
their shadows softened by the configuration of the rock, often shading
imperceptibly into the cloud-filled sky.

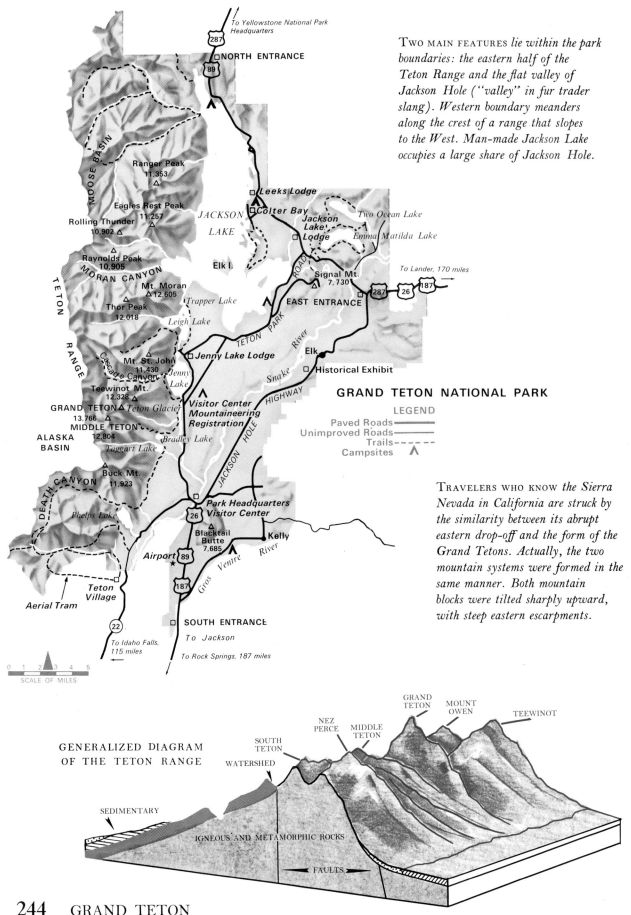

To Yellowstone National Park
Headquarters

NORTH ENTRANCE

MOOSE BASIN

Ranger Peak
11,353

Eagles Rest Peak
11,257

Rolling Thunder
10,902

JACKSON
LAKE

Leeks Lodge

Colter Bay

Jackson
Lake
Lodge

Two Ocean Lake

Emma Matilda Lake

Elk I.

Raynolds Peak
10,905

MORAN CANYON

Mt. Moran
12,605

Signal Mt.
7,730

To Lander, 170 miles

EAST ENTRANCE

287 26 187

Thor Peak
12,018

Trapper Lake

Leigh Lake

TETON

RANGE

Mt. St. John
11,430

Cascade Canyon

Jenny
Lake

Teewinot Mt.
12,328

GRAND TETON
13,766

Teton Glacier

MIDDLE TETON
12,804

ALASKA
BASIN

Bradley Lake

Taggart Lake

Jenny Lake Lodge

Elk

Historical Exhibit

TETON PARK ROAD

Snake River

GRAND TETON NATIONAL PARK

Visitor Center
Mountaineering
Registration

HIGHWAY

LEGEND
Paved Roads ——————
Unimproved Roads ——————
Trails --------
Campsites ⋀

JACKSON HOLE

DEATH CANYON

Buck Mt.
11,923

Phelps Lake

Park Headquarters
Visitor Center

26

Blacktail
Butte
7,685

Kelly

Gros Ventre River

Airport 89

187

Aerial Tram

Teton
Village

22

SOUTH ENTRANCE

To Jackson

To Idaho Falls,
115 miles

To Rock Springs, 187 miles

0 1 2 3 4 5
SCALE OF MILES

GRAND
TETON

MOUNT
OWEN

TEEWINOT

NEZ
PERCE

MIDDLE
TETON

SOUTH
TETON

GENERALIZED DIAGRAM
OF THE TETON RANGE

WATERSHED

SEDIMENTARY

IGNEOUS AND METAMORPHIC ROCKS

FAULTS

IN THE SHADOW OF THE TETON RANGE, *the Snake River begins its winding course to the Columbia River, 1,000 miles away.*

245

SNOWMOBILE PARTY HEADS FORTH *on an overland excursion. These popular vehicles open a new scenic world to visitors to the park, provide a means of reaching frozen lakes and ice-encrusted streams for fishing through the ice, and permit a half dozen dude ranches in the area to remain open through the winter. The little snowcats can only be driven on unplowed roads or along stake-marked snow trails, specially surveyed for such use. One snowmobile route covers more than a single day's drive and offers overnight accommodations at the midpoint.*

HIKERS' VIEW OF JACKSON HOLE *from the Amphitheater Lake Trail, which zigzags up from Jenny Lake through mountainside forest and steep-sloping meadows. The whole sweep of Jackson Hole is in full view through every opening until the trail flattens out on a high bench. Immediately below: Bradley and Taggart Lakes and in the distance, Blacktail Butte.*

MAGNET FOR MOUNTAINEERS

THE JAGGED SPIRES OF THE TETONS *attract mountain climbers from all over the world. First attempts in the 1870's to scale the Grand Teton failed, but by now several thousand mountaineers have entered their names in the log on the summit.*

There are at least 16 basic routes up the "Grand," ranging in difficulty from third to fifth-class climbs, in mountaineering language. The third-class climb cannot be made alone, and the fifth-class routes are attempted only by expert teams. Registration is required before climbs are attempted. A school at Jenny Lake trains novices in the basic techniques. The post-graduate exercise is a climb up one of the easier routes on the Grand.

The essence of mountaineering is the calculated conquest of a peak, not harrowing acrobatics. A few climbing techniques made safe by the use of simple but reliable tools will get a man to his goal in these most difficult of American peaks.

BASIC TOOLS OF MOUNTAINEERING

BECAUSE THEIR LIVES *literally depend on their gear, mountaineers use only the topmost quality pitons and fresh, pretested nylon rope.*

1. PITONS *are driven into rock cracks to anchor ropes. Of high-test metal, can resist pull of 10G's or sudden strain of 5G's if properly driven.*
2. CARABINER *is snap ring that clips to piton, acts as pulley for rapelling, belaying.*
3. HAMMER *is prime tool. Blunt end for driving pitons; sharp end to test strength of fractured rock, chip away unsafe rock for solid hold.*
4. CLEATS *on boots assure secure grip on narrow ledges.*

RAPELLING IS QUICKEST MEANS OF DESCENT. *Climber secures himself to one end of doubled rope passed through carabiner, lowers himself to firm footing, and retrieves his rope. Used at X-points on climbing map on opposite page.*

BELAYING IS USED *to get past tough spots. Man edging around rock is attached by rope to leader above him who is firmly anchored and ready to belay the fall of the climber should he slip. (Used at Z-points on the map.)*

FINGER-AND-TOE WORK *like this calls for mastery of climbing art; used at Y-points on the map. Leader of climbing party chooses the route with all members of party in mind. When he reaches safe point, he becomes belayer for next man behind him.*

CLIMBING MAP OF THE
GRAND TETON, NORTH FACE

*X—Rappel points
Y—Finger-and-toe climbs
Z—Difficult belays.*

E. N. DYE, FROM SIERRA CLUB'S "CLIMBER'S GUIDE TO TETON RANGE"

PRECISE KNOWLEDGE OF SUCCESSFUL ROUTES *is set out in books on often-climbed ranges. Sixteen routes lead to the summit of Grand Teton, some are numbered on this map.*

Fur-trade rendezvousing, *cattle rustling, sheep wars are among the dramatic events that have taken place in tranquil looking Jackson Hole. Fur traders assembled here in the 1830's in wary company with the Shoshones; after the supply of fur-bearing animals declined, cattle were run here—initially by rustlers who capitalized on the remoteness of the area and later by European promoters who were nearly wiped out by blizzards in the 1870's; in 1892, sheep were slaughtered by cattlemen in an attempt to keep them out of the Hole. Now the valley is a peaceful setting for dude ranchers and tourists.*

ANSEL ADAMS

Left to right: *Mount Moran (12,605 ft.), named for landscape painter Thomas Moran in 1872; Bivouac Peak (11,045 ft.), and Eagles Rest Peak (11,257 ft.). In foreground, Jackson Lake.*

250   GRAND TETON

5,000 ELK WINTERING IN SNOW-COVERED JACKSON HOLE. *Once nearly extinct, the elk (wapiti) are now almost more numerous than the winter range can support. The herds spend summer months in Yellowstone and migrate south in the fall, heading for lower and less forbidding area to spend the winter. En route between the two national parks, many are bagged by hunters who wait for them in the unprotected zone between.*

POWERFUL AND TRUCULENT BULL MOOSE *is best viewed from a reasonable distance. Moose usually summer in the higher mountains, but they may sometimes be seen browsing alder leaves around beaver ponds or grazing in the meadows.*

SPLIT-RAIL FENCING ALONG THE BYWAYS *emphasizes the "Western" atmosphere around Jackson Hole. This picturesque barrier keeps elk from invading nearby ranches.*

GRAND TETON   253

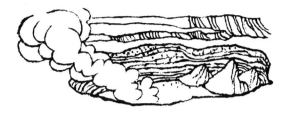

HAWAII VOLCANOES

HOME OF THE VOLCANO GODDESS

PARK FACTS: *Location:* Southeastern Hawaii. *Discovered:* By missionaries in 1830's. *Established:* Hawaii Nat. Park, Aug. 1, 1916; and Haleakala separated from it, 1961; renamed Hawaii Volcanoes. *Size:* 344 sq. mi. *Altitude:* Sea level to 13,680 ft. *Climate:* From semitropical to subarctic. *Season:* All year. *Visitors in 1968:* 918,000.

THE EIGHTEEN HAWAIIAN ISLANDS are actually the tips of a massive range of volcanic mountains that rise from the bottom of the Pacific. They formed slowly, in the way of shield volcanoes: Liquid lava erupted and spread in broad sheets; as these hardened to build up successive layers, great inverted saucers or "shields" took shape. Thus over the ages the mountains grew up from the ocean floor, until their peaks finally rose above the surface of the sea.

They were not all created at the same time. The big island of Hawaii is the youngest, and on it are found the only volcanoes in the range that are still active: Mauna Loa and Kilauea. These two are among the most exciting in existence, and their crests are the principal features of Hawaii Volcanoes National Park.

Mauna Loa, "Long Mountain," is in fact the biggest mountain in the world, although most of it is hidden under the waters of the Pacific. Its base is on the ocean floor, and the lower 18,000 feet of its elevation lie below the water. The summit is 13,680 feet above sea level, so its total size is astonishing: a mass 100 times that of Mount Shasta, a height more than 2,000 feet greater than that of Mount Everest.

Mauna Loa has a large crater or caldera, called Mokuaweoweo: Island of Lurid Burning. Within this great basin are several summit craters that have erupted in the past and partially covered the caldera floor with lava.

Although smaller than Mauna Loa, Kilauea gets even more attention because it is so accessible. Visitors can park their cars within 200 feet of its summit or drive all the way around the top on good roads. At some time in the past the mountaintop collapsed to form a small caldera, or cauldron, and within this basin

EFFERVESCENT FOUNTAIN OF FIRE *flares up 1,000 feet from the crater of Kilauea during the eruption of 1959. In the first stages of an eruption, fire fountains break through the crust, are followed by a flood of fiery lava.*

ROBERT WENKAM

are several craters, largest of which is called Halemaumau: House of Everlasting Fire. Prior to 1924, a lake of molten lava constantly rose and fell inside Halemaumau; and within recent years, the crater has provided some of the most dramatic demonstrations to be seen anywhere. Wild fountains spray upward, and lava pours out of cracks in the floor.

This is the legendary home of Pele, the Hawaiian goddess of volcanoes. She is gone a good deal, visiting other islands of the Pacific; but Hawaiians always know when she returns, because of renewed activity in Halemaumau.

Eruptions within the craters of Mauna Loa and Kilauea are relatively harmless, extremely exciting, and fascinating to watch—and thousands of spectators have looked in on them from the crater rims. But the eruptions also break out in other areas. Both of the volcanoes have huge fissures in their flanks, and when underground pressures grow great enough to force the lava out these openings, it starts a slow and deadly advance down the slopes toward the sea, destroying crops and villages in its path. In 1960 the village of Kapoho was buried.

The active interest of Hawaiian citizens in protecting and preserving their volcanoes led to establishment in 1916 of Hawaii National Park. It included not only portions of Mauna Loa and Kilauea but also part of Haleakala, on the island of Maui. In 1961 the Haleakala section became a separate national park, and the Mauna Loa-Kilauea, section was given its present name.

TWO GREAT VOLCANOES *dominate the park's terrain: Mauna Loa and Kilauea. Formed by gentle outpourings of lava over the centuries, they are shaped like inverted saucers. Within each massive crater (caldera) are smaller craters.*

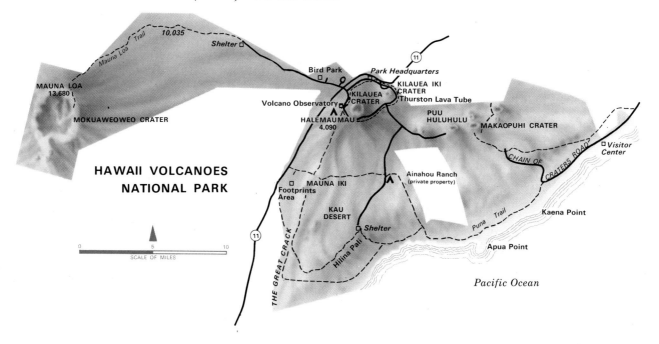

Long view across the caldera of Kilauea, sunk deep in the restless earth, to the flattened dome of Mauna Loa 25 miles away. The summit of Mauna Loa is 10,000 feet higher than that of Kilauea.

ROBERT WENKAM

HAWAII VOLCANOES 257

A RIVER OF MOLTEN LAVA *once swept through this tube and poured out of Kilauea Iki (the "smaller"). As the lava streamed out of the side of the volcano, it baked its own conduit of rock. The Thurston Lava Tube is reached by a short trail from the road that passes through a lush jungle.*

A CRATER WITHIN A CRATER, *Halemaumau is the active part of Kilauea. From the floor of this oval-shaped vent, ½ mile across and several hundred feet deep, have roared spectacular fire fountains and lava flows, the most recent in 1967 and 1968. Lava brims over the rim of the inner crater and flows onto the floor of the great caldera, whose encircling walls contain it.*

HAWAII VOLCANOES 259

DEVASTATED BY THE ERUPTION OF 1959, *the skeletal remains of an ohia forest stand as bleak reminders of the destructive power of a volcano. The dead forest is located to the leeward of a cinder cone formed by this eruption.*

SOLIDIFIED INTO SWIRLING FLOW PATTERNS, *the lava that poured out of Kilauea in ages past covers a large area in the park. Best seen in the Kau desert where it is not covered with vegetation. The crust is brittle, collapses under foot.*

ALONG THE SHORELINE HIGHWAY, *waves smash against the cliffs formed of chunks of lava and wrinkled layers of old lava flow. The rock wall and palm trees mark the site of an abandoned settlement at Kamoamoa.*

A TANGLE OF FERNS, *some as large as small trees, share a jungle luxuriance with the scrubby ohia trees in the eastern part of the park. The ohia blossoms are noted for their beauty. Known as* lehua, *these scarlet, feathery blooms are the official flower of the island of Hawaii.*

ANSEL ADAMS

HAWAII VOLCANOES　263

ROBERT WENKAM

HALEAKALA

THE MOON ON EARTH

PARK FACTS. *Location:* Central Maui, Hawaiian Islands. *Established:* Part of Hawaii Nat. Park, Aug. 1,1916; separate status, July 1, 1961. *Size:* 44 sq. mi. *Altitude:* Sea level to 10,023 ft. *Climate:* Cool, windy. *Season:* All year. *Visitors. 1968:* 132,700.

Most of the eastern part of the Hawaiian island of Maui is a weirdly beautiful wasteland created by the fiery outpourings of a huge, now dormant volcano. The sleeping giant is called Haleakala: "House of the Sun."

At sea level the great mountain is 33 miles long and 24 miles wide. The elevation at its summit is 10,023 feet—high enough for snow flurries in winter. From the glassed-in Puu Ulaula Observatory at the top, visitors can see as far as 130 miles on clear days. In one direction the slope drops away to the sea; in another, the distant peaks of Mauna Loa and Mauna Kea, on the island of Hawaii, are visible. And in the foreground is the curious landscape of the vast Haleakala Crater, its floor 3,000 feet below the summit, its circumference 21 miles.

The bowl is pocked with numerous smaller craters and studded with cones formed of the cinders, ash, and spatter blown from volcanic vents. The tallest of these multicolored forms, Puu O Maui, rises 1,000 feet above the surrounding level.

Although Haleakala has not been active since the mid-eighteenth century, it is considered dormant rather than extinct; one indication that it is not dead is the earthquake activity recorded periodically on Maui.

There are several good vantage points along the rim drive to the summit, including Leleiwi and Kalahaku overlooks and the Haleakala Visitor Center. All look across to the peak called Hanakauhi, "Maker of Mists," which is often wreathed in clouds.

Most of the crater is nearly barren of plant life, but in the northeast corner is a surprise—an oasis of trees, grasses, and ferns. This spot receives 200 inches of rain a year, and the soil conditions are right for vegetation. A few plants

THE WEST WALL OF HALEAKALA CRATER, *viewed from the visitor center, slopes 2,500 feet down into the caldera, its surface covered with smooth cinders, blown on top of the original rocky wall by trade winds. Clouds are billowing in from Koolau Gap, one of the two valleys within the caldera.*

265

exist elsewhere in the crater; one is the rare silversword, found only on the islands of Maui and Hawaii. When this odd plant matures (within 7 to 40 years) with a tall, fat stalk, it bears a hundred or more small, purplish flowers. After blooming, it dies.

Two main trails lead into Haleakala Crater, where they branch into a network that totals about 30 miles. Hikers and horseback riders will find many exotic formations, including lava tubes, and a colorful part of the trail called Pele's Paintpot. Stone monuments left by the early Hawaiians are also of special interest.

In the Hosmer Grove and Paliku areas of the park, there are birds in surprising number and variety. A dozen kinds of introduced birds share the sanctuary with natives; the rare nene (Hawaiian goose) is being reintroduced to the island. No mammals are native to the park, but there are some immigrant pigs, goats, and smaller animals.

Haleakala was included (along with Mauna Loa and Kilauea, on the island of Hawaii) in Hawaii National Park when it was established in 1916. In 1961, a division of that park resulted in redesignating the Mauna Loa-Kilauea section as Hawaii Volcanoes National Park and the Maui section as Haleakala National Park.

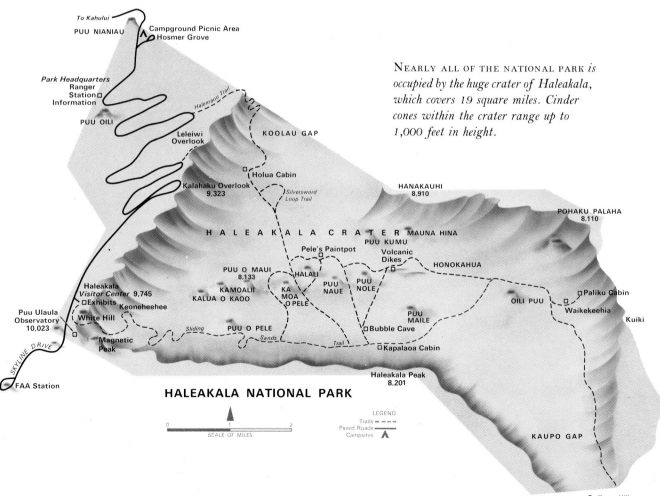

NEARLY ALL OF THE NATIONAL PARK *is occupied by the huge crater of Haleakala, which covers 19 square miles. Cinder cones within the crater range up to 1,000 feet in height.*

HALEAKALA NATIONAL PARK

SCALE OF MILES

LEGEND
Trails
Paved Roads
Campsites

THE FULL IMMENSITY OF THE CALDERA, *a great basin 7 miles by 3, can best be seen from the air. From its floor rise cinder cones that last erupted centuries ago—and may again some day.*

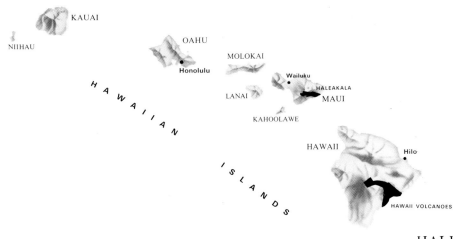

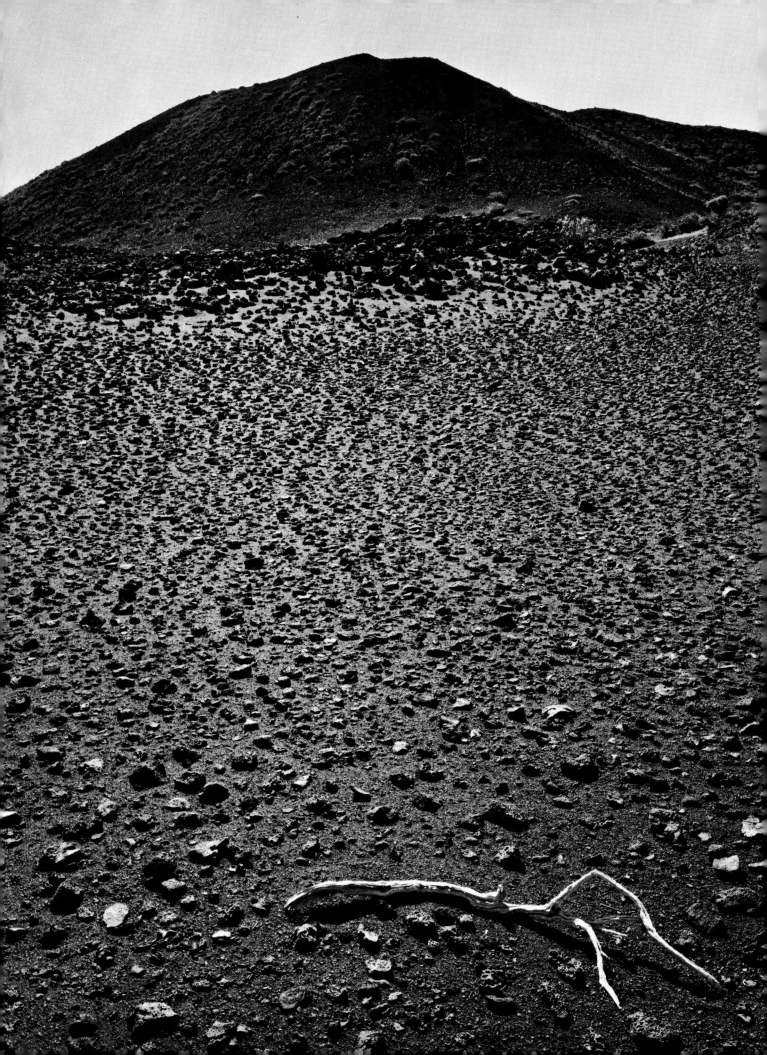

SHADOWS CAST BY CLOUDS ON THE RUGGED TERRAIN *add greater visual drama to Kipahulu Valley. In far distance is majestic form of Mauna Kea on Island of Hawaii.*

EERIE AND FORBIDDING, *cinder-strewn surface of the crater has the look of another planet. Fist-size cinders formed by sudden cooling of lava expelled into the air.*

HALEAKALA **269**

MAN IS DWARFED BY THE MOON-LIKE *landscape within the vast crater. Nearly 30 miles of trail weave a path among the cinder cones and other volcanic curiosities. Hikers can spend up to 4 days in the basin without retracing.*

GRAINS OF IRON OXIDE LAVA *that form the cinder cones reflect the sun in a changing array of color. Each grain reflects the sun's rays differently at different hours of the day, creating scenes that range from monotonous to brightly colored landscapes.*

KIPAHULU VALLEY *has virgin forest of rare native plants above 3,000 feet.*
At lower elevations, the seven pools of Kipahulu stair-step their way
down to the sea.

PARK FACTS

DIGEST FOR THE TRAVELER, FACT COLLECTOR

Western Parks Directory

For up-to-date information, prospective visitors to the parks should write to one or all of the following agencies. Address letters to:

1. *Superintendent* of the park at the address below for data on public accommodations, visitor activities, free maps, park regulations, current weather and road conditions, etc.

2. The *Natural History Association* at the same address as the park superintendent (unless otherwise indicated) for lists of books, leaflets, maps, and color slides obtainable by mail.

3. The *Manager* of the business concession under contract to the Park Service for information about resort accommodations, package tours, or concessioner-operated activities. Note that some concessioners move to a different address for the winter.

BRYCE CANYON NATIONAL PARK

Bryce Canyon, Utah 84717
—*Concessioner:*
  The Utah Parks Company
  Cedar City, Utah 84720

CANYONLANDS NATIONAL PARK

Moab, Utah 84532
—*Concessioner:*
  None in park. Motels on outskirts.

CARLSBAD CAVERNS NATIONAL PARK

P.O. Box 1598
Carlsbad, N. Mex. 88220
—*Concessioner:*
  None in park.

CRATER LAKE NATIONAL PARK

Crater Lake, Ore. 97604
—*Concessioner:*
  Crater Lake Lodge, Inc.
  Crater Lake, Ore. 97604

GLACIER NATIONAL PARK

West Glacier, Mont. 59936
—*Concessioner:*
  Glacier Park, Inc.
  (May 15-Sept. 15) East Glacier Park, Mont. 59343
  (Sept. 15-May 15) 1735 E. Ft. Lowell Rd.
  Tucson, Ariz. 95717

GRAND TETON NATIONAL PARK

Moose, Wyo. 83012
—*Concessioner:*
  • Grand Teton Lodge Co.
   Jackson, Wyo. 83001
  • Signal Mt. Lodge
   Moran, Wyo. 83013
  • Leek's Lodge Inc.
   Moran, Wyo 83013
  • Triangle Guest Ranch
   Moose, Wyo. 83012
  • Elbo Guest Ranch
   Moose, Wyo. 83012

GRAND CANYON NATIONAL PARK

Grand Canyon, Ariz. 86023
—Natural History Association
  P.O. Box 219
  Grand Canyon, Ariz. 86023
—*Concessioner—South Rim:*
  Fred Harvey, Inc.
  Grand Canyon, Ariz. 86023
—*Concessioner—North Rim:*
  The Utah Parks Company
  Cedar City, Utah 84720

HALEAKALA NATIONAL PARK

P.O. Box 456
Kahului
Maui, Hawaii 96732
—*Concessioner:*
  None in park.

HAWAII VOLCANOES NATIONAL PARK

Hawaii Volcanoes National Park
Hawaii 96718
—*Concessioner:*
  Volcano House
  Hawaii Volcanoes National Park
  Hawaii 96718

KINGS CANYON NATIONAL PARK

Three Rivers, Calif. 93271
—*Concessioner:*
  Sequoia & Kings Canyon National Parks Co.
  Sequoia National Park, Calif. 93271

LASSEN VOLCANIC NATIONAL PARK

Mineral, Calif. 96063
—Loomis Museum Association
  Lassen Volcanic National Park
  Mineral, Calif. 96063
—*Concessioner:*
  Lassen National Park Co.
  Manzanita Lake, Calif. 96060

MESA VERDE NATIONAL PARK

Mesa Verde National Park
Colo. 81330

—*Concessioner:*
Mesa Verde Company
P.O. Box 277
Mancos, Colo. 81328

MOUNT McKINLEY NATIONAL PARK

Alaska Cluster Office
P.O. Box 2252
Anchorage, Alaska 99501
—*Concessioner:*
• McKinley Park Hotel
McKinley, Alaska 99755
(Oct. 1–April 30):
• McKinley National Park Co.
1735 E. Ft. Lowell Rd.
Tucson, Ariz. 85717

MOUNT RAINIER NATIONAL PARK

Longmire, Wash. 98397
—*Concessioner:*
Rainier National Park Co.
P.O. Box 1136
Tacoma, Wash. 98400

NORTH CASCADES NATIONAL PARK

Sedro Wooley, Wash. 98248
—*Concessioner:*
None in park. For information on nearby accommodations, write to the county chambers of commerce:
• Whatcom County
Bellingham, Wash. 98225
• Skagit County
Mount Vernon, Wash. 98273
• Snohomish County
Everett, Wash. 98201
• Chelan County
Wenatchee, Wash. 98801
• Okanogan County
Okanogan, Wash. 98840

OLYMPIC NATIONAL PARK

600 East Park Avenue
Port Angeles, Wash. 98362
—*Concessioner:*
For information about concession-operated cabins, lodges, and trailer parks at Sol Duc Springs, Lake Crescent, La Push, or Kalaloch, write to the park superintendent.
For information about accommodations outside the park, write to the Olympic Peninsula Resort and Hotel Association, Colman Ferry Terminal, Seattle, Wash. 98104

PETRIFIED FOREST NATIONAL PARK

Holbrook, Ariz. 86025
—*Concessioner:*
None in park. For accommodations on outskirts of park write:
• Rainbow Forest Lodge
P.O. Box N
Holbrook, Ariz. 86025

• Painted Desert Oasis
Holbrook, Ariz. 86025

REDWOOD NATIONAL PARK

Crescent City, Calif. 95531
—*Concessioner:*
None in park itself, but write to state parks within the boundaries.

ROCKY MOUNTAIN NATIONAL PARK

P.O. Box 1080
Estes Park, Colo. 80517
—Rocky Mountain Nature Association
P.O. Box 147
Estes Park, Colo. 80517
—*Concessioner:*
None in park. For accommodations outside park, write to the chambers of commerce in:
Estes Park, Colo. 80517
Grand Lake, Colo. 80447

SEQUOIA NATIONAL PARK

Three Rivers, Calif. 93271
—*Concessioner:*
Sequoia & Kings Canyon National Parks Co.
Sequoia National Park, Calif. 93262

YELLOWSTONE NATIONAL PARK

Yellowstone National Park
Wyo. 82190
—Yellowstone Library and Museum Association
P.O. Box 117
Yellowstone National Park, Wyo. 82190
—*Concessioner:*
Yellowstone Park Co.
Yellowstone National Park
Wyo. 82190
—For Fishing Bridge Trailer Village:
Hamilton Stores, Inc.
West Yellowstone, Mont. 59758
Winter address: P.O. Box 1230
Santa Monica, Calif. 90406

YOSEMITE NATIONAL PARK

P.O. Box 577
Yosemite National Park, Calif. 95389
—Natural History Association
P.O. Box 545
Yosemite National Park, Calif. 95389
—*Concessioner:*
Yosemite Park and Curry Co.
Yosemite National Park, Calif. 95389

ZION NATIONAL PARK

Springdale, Utah 84767
—*Concessioner:*
The Utah Parks Co.
Cedar City, Utah 84720

Seasonal Accommodation Guide

PARK	PUBLIC CAMPING, SEASON	PUBLIC CAMPING, NO. CAMPS	PUBLIC CAMPING, NO. SITES	PUBLIC CAMPING, LIMIT STAY	PUBLIC CAMPING, TRAILERS	CONCESSIO RESOR SEASO
MT. McKINLEY	June 1-Sept. 10	7	203	5 or 15 Days	15-ft. Unit; No Hookups	May 1-Sept. 30
NORTH CASCADES	Apr. 1-Oct. 15	20	193	14 Days; Winter: 30	None	Some All Year
OLYMPIC	May-Oct.; Some All Year	18	947	14 Days	No Hookups; Small at Most Camps	Some All Year
MT. RAINIER	June-Sept.; Sunshine Pt.: All Year	9	856	14 Days	All Camps; No Hookups	May-Oct.
CRATER LAKE	July 1-Sept. 30	4	290	14 Days	All Camps; No Hookups	June 15-Sept. 15
REDWOOD	June-Labor Day	4 (State Administered)	349	30 Days; Summer: 14	26 ft. Limit; No Hookups	None
LASSEN VOLCANIC	May-Oct.	8	545	14 Days	Most Camps; No Hookups	June 15-Labor Day
YOSEMITE	May-Sept. 15; Camp 4: All Year	23	2,576	14 Days; Valley (June-July): 7; Winter: 30	Most Camps; No Hookups	All Year in Valley
SEQUOIA	June-Oct.; Some All Year	9	842	14 Days; Winter: 30	3 Camps Only; No Hookups	May-Oct.; Camp All Year
KINGS CANYON	May-Oct.	8	848	14 Days	Cedar Grove Nos. 3, 4; Azalea Camp	May-Oct.
GRAND CANYON North rim	May-Oct.	2	78	14 Days	Most Camps	May 15-Oct. 15
GRAND CANYON South rim	All Year	7	421	14 Days	Most Camps; Hookups S. Rim Village	All Year
BRYCE CANYON	May 15-Oct. 15	2	225	14 Days	North Camp Only	Lodge: Mid-June-I Day. Inn: May 9-O
ZION	So. Camp: All Yr. Watchman Camp: May-Sept.	2	430	May 15-Sept. 15: 14 Days	Both Camps; No Hookups	Lodge: Mid-June-I Day. Inn: May 10-
CANYONLANDS	All Year	2 (Dry Camp; Island in the Sky)	39	14 Days	No Hookups	None
PETRIFIED FOREST	All Year	Camping Only in Holbrook and Distant National Forests			None	None
MESA VERDE	Apr.-Oct.	1	475	June-Sept. 1: 14 Days	Designated Camps Only; No Hookups	May 25-Oct. 15
CARLSBAD CAVERNS	All Year	None in Park				All Year
ROCKY MOUNTAIN	May-Oct.; Aspenglen: All Year	8	950	July-Aug.: 14 Days	Most Camps; No Hookups	
GLACIER	June-Sept.	17	1,276	July-Aug.: 14 Days	All Camps but Sprague Crk.; No Hookups	May 15-Sept. 15
YELLOWSTONE	June-Sept.; Mammoth: Apr.-Oct.	15	2,437	July-Labor Day: 14 Days	Most Camps; No Hookup	Mid-May-Mid-Oct.
GRAND TETON	May-Oct.	6	952	14 Days; Jenny Lake: 10 Days	All Camps but Jenny Lk.; No Hookups	Feb.-Oct.; Elbo Gu Ranch: All Year
HAWAII VOLCANOES	All Year	3 (Plus 2 Hikers' Cabins)	22 Plus Groups	7 Days	2 Camps Only	All Year
HALEAKALA	All Year	1	5 (3 Cabins, 12 Bunks ea., Advance Reservations)	Cabins Only: 3 Days	Parking Near Camp Only; No Hookups	All Year

FOR RESERVATIONS, SEE DIRECTORY, PAGE 274

winter

CESSIONER, CAMPS	CONCESSIONER, MOTELS/HOTELS	CONCESSIONER, CABINS	NONCONCESSIONER, ACCOMMODATIONS	CONCESSIONER, CAMPS/LOCALE	TRAILER FACILITIES	RESORTS, LOCALE
None	Yes	None	Camp Denali (Outside Pk.)	None	None	None
None	Nearby	Yes	Yes	None	None	Inside Park and Nearby
None	Yes	Yes	Nearby	Kalaloch, El Wha	Nearby	Nearby: Port Angeles
None	Yes	None	None	Sunshine Point	Nearby	Nearby
None	Yes	Yes	None	None	Nearby	Nearby
(Trailer)	Nearby	None	None	Yes	Yes	Nearby
None	Yes	Yes	Nearby	None	Nearby	Nearby: Mineral
ountry	Yes	Valley	Wawona Village, El Portal	Valley	Valley	Wawona; Valley
None	Yes	Yes	None	Yes	Nearby	Giant Forest
None	Yes	Yes	Wilsonia Village	None	None	Wilsonia Village
None	Yes	Yes	None	None	None	None
None	Yes	Yes	None	All Year	None	Yes
None	Yes	Yes	None	None	None	None
Trailer Cts. Near Pk.	Yes	Yes	None	South Camp	Nearby	Nearby: Springdale
Monticello, Moab	Nearby	Nearby	None	All Year	All Year	None
None	Nearby	None	None			Nearby
None	Yes	Yes	None	None	None	None
None	None	None	Chaparral Pk: 22 Campsites			
Estes Park Village	Nearby		None	Nearby	None	Nearby
None	Yes	Yes	Lake McDonald	None	None	None
Trailer Hookups: Fish-idge Trailer Vil.)	Yes	Yes	None	None	None	Mammoth Motor Inn
Trailer Hookups: Bay Trlr. Vil.)	Yes	Yes	Several	None	None	Nearby: Jackson
Military Camp	Yes	Yes	None	All Year	All Year	All Year
None	Nearby, toward Kahului	None	None	All Year	All Year	Nearby

Seasonal Activity Guide

PARK	SEASON	TOTAL LENGTH, HIKING TRAILS	PACKING	HORSEBACK RIDING	BICYCLING	FISHING
MT. McKINLEY	June 1-Sept. 1	8 Miles	From Lignite	None	None	Lake, Stream; No Li
NORTH CASCADES	Apr. 1-Oct. 15	345 Miles	Yes	Yes	None	Lake, Stream; Lic.
OLYMPIC	May-Oct.; Limited All Year	Over 600 Miles	From Forks, Port Angeles	None	None	Lake, Stream; No Li
MT. RAINIER	All Year	300 Miles	None	None	Permitted on Roads; No Rentals	Lake, Stream; No Li
CRATER LAKE	July-Sept.	6 Miles	Yes	None	Permitted on Roads; No Rentals	Stream: July 15-Se Lake: If Trail Ope No Lic. Req.
REDWOOD	June-Labor Day	Approx. 75 Miles	None	None	None	Lic. Req.
LASSEN VOLCANIC	May-Oct.	150 Miles	Summit Lake; Drakesbad	Drakesbad	None	Most Lakes; Lic. R
YOSEMITE	Valley: All Year; High Ctry.: Summer	Over 700 Miles	High Sierra Loop; John Muir Trail	Yes; Four Stables	Permitted on Roads; Rentals	Lakes, Rivers, Stre Lic. Req.
SEQUOIA	June-Oct.	600 Miles	Giant Forest and elsewhere	Giant Forest	None	Streams, May-Oct. Lic. Req.
KINGS CANYON	June-Oct.	400 Miles	Grant Grove; Cedar Grove	Grant Grove; Cedar Grove	None	Streams, Lakes; Li
GRAND CANYON North rim	May-Oct.	31 Miles (Half in Canyon)	Concessioner Mules: Reserve in Advance	Summer Only	Permitted on Main Roads; No Rentals	Streams; Lic. Req.
GRAND CANYON South rim	All Year					
BRYCE	May 15-Oct. 15	61 Miles	None	Yes	None	None
ZION	All Year	155 Miles	None	Yes	None	Stream; Lic. Req.
CANYONLANDS	All Year	15 Miles	None	None	None	None
PETRIFIED FOREST	All Year	Long Hikes; Register	None	None	None	None
MESA VERDE	May-Oct. 15	Few Short Trails; Permit Required	None	Guided	None	None
CARLSBAD CAVERNS	All Year	13 Miles, Underground	None	None	None	None
ROCKY MOUNTAIN	May-Oct.	300 Miles	None	Yes; Rental	None	Streams, Lakes; Li
GLACIER	June-Sept.	1,000 Miles	Yes	Rentals; Guides Req'd. for Trips	Permitted; No Rentals	Streams, Lakes; N Lic. Req.
YELLOWSTONE	June-Sept. 15	1,000 Miles	Yes	Rentals; Guides Req'd. for Trips	None	Streams, Lakes; N Lic. Req.
GRAND TETON	May-Oct.	200 Miles	Yes	Yes	None	Streams, Lakes; L
HAWAII VOLCANOES	All Year	160 Miles	None	None	Permitted; No Rentals	Ocean: Halape to Boundary
HALEAKALA	All Year	32 Miles	Regular Trails	1 to 4-Day Trips; Guides with Rentals Only	None	None

FOR ACCOMMODATIONS, SEE PAGE 276

winter

BOATING	SWIMMING	ROCK, ICE CLIMBING	GUIDED TOURS	SEASON	SKIING	SNOWMOBILING	ICE-SKATING, ETC.
Rentals; No Motors	Wonder Lk.; Horseshoe Lk.	Yes; Register	Charter Bus	Closed Sept.-May	None	None	None
Yes	Low Temp.: Not Advised	Yes; Register	Plane, Boat	Open	Nearby	Yes	None
als; Lk. Crescent ching	Sol Duc Hot Springs	Yes; Register	Gray Line	Late Dec.-Mar.	Hurricane Ridge	Unplowed Roads Only	Heart of the Hills
Rentals; Designated s Only	None	Rock: School; Ice: All Year; Register	Hikes, Nat. Walks	Dec.-May	Paradise (Weekends Only); X-Ctry. Trails	Designated Areas Only; Register	None
al, Rowboats Only	None	None	Bus, Launch	Oct.-May	X-Country	When Snow Depth over 2 ft.; Register	None
None	In Streams	None	None	None	None	None	None
als; Manzanita, Butte No Power	Most Lakes	None	Naturalist Walks	Mid. Dec.-Mid. Apr.	Ski Area; X-Country	Unplowed Park Roads Only	Manzanita Lake
gnated Lakes Only; Power	Pools: Valley	Rock: Valley: School, Guides; Register. Ice: Lyell Gl.	Tram, Bus, Horseback, Hiking	Mid. Dec.-Mid. Apr.	Badger Pass; X-Country	Glacier Pt. Rd., Tioga Rd.	Curry Village; Sleighing
None	Low Temp.: Not Advised	Register	Naturalist Walks; (Crystal Cave)	Dec.-Apr.	Wolverton; X-Country	None	Lodge Pole, Dec.-Feb.
None	Low Temp.: Not Advised	None	Grant Grove, Cedar Grove	Nov.-Apr.	X-Country	None	Snow Play, Grant Grove
None	Phantom Ranch	None	Mule, Horseback, Charter Cars	Closed / Nov.-May 10	None	None	None
None	None	Prohibited	Bus, Trail	Dec.-Apr.	None	None	None
None	Zion Lodge Pool	Rock Only; Register	Naturalist Walks	South Camp	None	Some	None
None	None	None	Jeep	All Year			
None	None	None	Naturalist Walks	All Year	None	None	None
None	None	None	Bus, Walks	Oct. 15-May 15	None	None	None
None	None	None	Naturalist Walks	All Year	None	None	None
None	None	Yes; Guide Service	Bus, Auto, Naturalist Walks	Mid. Dec.-Mid. Apr.	Hidden Valley; X-Ctry.	West Side of Park	Yes
nches; Rentals; Some ters, No Power	Lk. McDonald, but Not Recommended	Not Recommended	Naturalist Walks	Sept. 10-June 15	X-Ctry Only; Hazardous	75 miles of Road; Permit Req.	None
tals; Private Craft er 40 ft.	None	None	Naturalist Walks	Dec.-Mar.	X-Ctry Only; Register	Dec.-Mar.; Tours; Register	None
tals; Snake R. Trips	Colter Bay; Jackson Lk. Lodge Pool	Rock: School; Rock, Ice: Register	Bus, Lake Cruise, River Raft, Walks	Dec.-Mar.	X-Country; Ski Area Nearby	Tours; Permit Req.	Ice Fishing
None	None	None	Bus				
None	Kipahula Addition	Rock Climbing	None	Dec.-Feb.	None	None	None

Historical Chronology

1400's   Apache Indian tribe moves into area of Carlsbad Caverns.

1500's   Pecos River area explored by Spanish conquistadores.

1540   Don Lopez de Cardenas discovers the Grand Canyon.

——— 1700 ———

1700's   Paiute tribe claims Zion region.

1720   Blackfoot Indians penetrate Glacier area, hold for a century.

1765   Don Juan Maria de Rivera leads first official Spanish expedition into Mesa Verde area.

mid-1770's   Spanish traders penetrate southwestern Colorado.

1774   Spanish sea Captain Juan Perez discovers Olympic Mountains; called them *La Sierra de la Santa Rosalia.*

1776   Zion area discovered by Escalante-Dominguez party of Spanish padres. Escalante and Dominguez camp at foot of Mesa Verde.

1788   English Captain John Meares names dominant Olympic peak Mount Olympus.

1790   Hawaiian volcano Kilauea has violent steam explosion.

1792   Captain Vancouver sights Mount Rainier while sailing in Puget Sound; names it for his friend Rear Admiral Peter Rainier.

——— 1800 ———

1800's   Ranchers in the Pecos River area venture into the mountainous area near Carlsbad Caverns; refer to caverns as Bat Cave.

1800-50   Trappers use Bryce Canyon.

1803   United States acquires Rocky Mountain area as part of Louisiana Purchase.

1806   Meriwether Lewis reaches point 30 miles from Glacier Park area.

1807   John Colter of Lewis and Clark party discovers Jackson Hole; leaves expedition to explore Yellowstone.

1811   Astorians cross Grand Teton range.

1819   Grand Teton Mountains named by party of French-Canadian trappers.

——— 1820 ———

1820's   First missionaries arrive in Hawaiian Islands.

1821   Mexico wins independence from Spain. Mesa Verde becomes Mexican territory.

1826   Jedediah Smith leads party of 16 through Utah's valleys to Virgin River.

1829   Lake and valley in Grand Tetons named for David Jackson, mountain man. Antonio Armijo blazes trail from Santa Fe to the Pueblo of Los Angeles through Mesa Verde.

1833   Captain Joseph Walker expedition party crosses Sierra, probably enters Yosemite. Dr. William Fraser Tolmie and party of five Indians explore Mount Rainier area.

——— 1840 ———

1840   Fur trade in Grand Teton area begins decline; ends in 1860's.

1843-44   John C. Fremont explores Zion.

1845   Fremont's third western expedition travels along Kern River in Sequoia-Kings Canyon area.

1847   Mormons migrate en masse to Great Salt Lake valley.

1848   United States signs Treaty of Guadalupe Hidalgo, takes possession of Mesa Verde and Grand Canyon.

1849   United States Department of Interior created to be responsible for national resources, including national parks.

WESTERN NATIONAL PARKS IN ORDER OF FOUNDING

1. Yellowstone, 1872	9. Rocky Mountain, 1915	17. Carlsbad Caverns, 1930
2. Sequoia, 1890	10. Lassen Volcanic, 1916	18. Olympic, 1938
3. General Grant, 1890*	11. Hawaii, 1916***	19. Kings Canyon, 1940
4. Yosemite, 1890**	12. Mount McKinley, 1917	20. Haleakala, 1961
5. Mount Rainier, 1899	13. Grand Canyon, 1919	21. Petrified Forest, 1962
6. Crater Lake, 1902	14. Zion, 1919	22. Canyonlands, 1964
7. Mesa Verde, 1906	15. Bryce Canyon, 1928	23. North Cascades, 1968
8. Glacier, 1910	16. Grand Teton, 1929	24. Redwood, 1968

*Incorporated into Kings Canyon, 1940.
**Established as a state-operated park in 1864.
***Became two national parks—Hawaii Volcanoes and Haleakala—in 1961.

1850

1850-70 Mormon scouts explore Bryce Canyon area. Hale Tharp settles at Three Rivers (Sequoia-Kings Canyon).

1851 Mariposa Battalion enters Yosemite Valley to subdue the Sierra Indian tribe. Lt. Lorenzo Sitgreaves explores northern Arizona, reports "stone trees."

mid-1800's Lassen Peak used as a landmark by Peter Lassen (California pioneer from Denmark) when he piloted emigrants from Humboldt, Nevada, into the Sacramento Valley.

1853 John Wesley Hillman is first white man to see what is now known as Crater Lake; names it Deep Blue Lake. Railroad survey party crosses Glacier mountain range.

1855 James Mason Hutchings leads first tourist party into Yosemite.

1856 Clark's Station—now known as Wawona—established in Yosemite by Galen Clark. Sketches of Yosemite from 1855 trip (drawn by Thomas Ayres) appear in *California Magazine* and attract visitors from all over the United States.

1857 First serious assault on Mount Rainier by Lt. A. V. Kautz, Dr. O. R. Craig, Indian guide, and four soldiers.

1858 Potwisha Indians lead Hale Tharp up to Indian Trail under Moro Rock to the big trees (Sequoia-Kings Canyon). Nephi Johnson discovers Zion Canyon.

1859 Joel Estes and son Milton see Rocky Mountain park area. Prof. J. S. Newberry, geologist with the Macomb expedition, climbs Mesa Verde, provides first printed description.

1859-60 Brigadier General W. F. Reynolds leads exploration party into Yellowstone area; writes report complete with illustrated map.

1860

1860 Estes family settles in valley in Rocky Mountains.

1861 Canadian boundary party surveys Glacier area.

1862 Party of prospectors led by Chauncey Nye stumble on lake in a crater, name it Blue Lake. Joseph Thomas discovers General Grant Grove and General Grant Tree.

1864 National grant signed by Lincoln to make Yosemite a recreational area; becomes the first state park.

1865 Two soldiers "discover" Crater Lake, name it Lake Majesty.

1867 Griff Evans acquires Estes claim in Rocky Mountains.

1868 Major John Wesley Powell makes first successful ascent of Longs Peak in Rocky Mountains. John Muir comes to Yosemite area to herd sheep.

1869 Major Powell makes first successful transit of Grand Canyon. Visitors from Jacksonville see lake in a crater, name it Crater Lake. Reynolds report on Yellowstone published.

1870

1870 Nineteen men in Washburn, Langford, Doane expedition explore Yellowstone; return to Montana and propose area be made into a national park. Major Powell expedition explores Bryce Canyon. Crest of Mount Rainier reached by Hazard Stevens and P. B. Van Trump.

1871 Scientific and military expedition directed by Dr. Ferdinand V. Hayden explores Yellowstone.

1872 First known photographs of Grand Tetons taken from west by W. H. Jackson. Major Powell visits Zion, calls N. fork of Virgin River "Mukuntuweap" and E. fork "Parunuweap." Yellowstone National Park established.

1874 First photographs made of the Mesa Verde cliff dwellings by W. H. Jackson. First Mormon settlements established in Bryce Canyon.

1875 Ebenezer Bryce settles in Bryce Canyon.

1877 Chief Joseph and his Nez Perce Indians retreat through Yellowstone.

1878 Settlement of Arizona begins.

1879 Artist Thomas Moran paints the Grand Tetons. A trapper, James Wolverton, discovers General Sherman Tree.

1880

1880's Tourist travel to Grand Canyon begins. Muir writes in *Century Illustrated Monthly Magazine* on need to preserve Yosemite. Rocky Mountains mining boom is on; Lulu City, Dutchtown, and Teller established.

1881 Mauna Loa erupts; lava enters outskirts of Hilo.

1883 Atlantic and Pacific Railway (now Santa Fe) completed. James Longmire discovers warm mineral springs during summit climb of Mount Rainier.

1884 Longmire constructs first building (near present park headquarters) on Mount Rainier. First settlers arrive in Grand Tetons; villages of Jackson, Wilson, and Moran established.

1885 William G. Steel of Kansas sees Crater Lake and determines to preserve it.

1887 Senator Benjamin Harrison, Indiana, introduces a bill to make the Grand Canyon a national park.

1888   Richard Wetherill and Charles Mason dis-
        cover the Mesa Verde's Cliff Palace, Spruce
        Tree House and Square Tower House. Wil-
        liam Steel plants 37 fingerling rainbow trout
        in Crater Lake.

1889   Marias Pass, used by Great Northern, ex-
        plored by John F. Stevens.

1889-90 First major exploration of Olympics by
        Press Party led by James Cristie and
        Captain Charles Barnes.

1890   Sequoia National Park, General Grant Na-
        tional Park, Yosemite National Park are all
        established. Longmire and sons push crude
        road through and build small hotel at Long-
        mire's Springs on Mount Rainier. Copper
        ore discovered in Glacier area; short mining
        boom collapses when ore found unprofitable.

1891   Town of Tropic founded in Bryce Canyon.
        Swedish scientist Gustaf Nordenskiold con-
        ducts first scientific excavations of the Mesa
        Verde. Sierra Club organized; John Muir
        and others determine to fight for big Kings
        Canyon.

1892   Hotel built at Grandview Point in Grand
        Canyon.

1893   Gun battle between settlers and horse thieves
        at Cunningham homestead in Grand Tetons.
        President Benjamin Harrison establishes
        Grand Canyon Forest Preserve.

1894   Efforts underway to preserve Mount Rainier
        area. Lacey Act passed to "protect the birds
        and animals in Yellowstone National Park
        and punish crimes in said park."

1896   Federal law enacted prohibiting removal of
        petrified wood from the Petrified Forest area.
        W. A. Dickey prospects in the region of
        Mount McKinley.

1897   Olympic Forest Reserve established.

1899   Mount Rainier National Park established.

1900

1900   Colorado Cliff Dwellings Association in-
        corporates and starts work to get park bill
        in Congress.

1901   Santa Fe Lines completes track to South Rim
        of Grand Canyon.

1902   Crater Lake National Park established. Al-
        fred H. Brooks and D. L. Raeburn of United
        States Geological Survey study geology of
        Alaska Range. Brooks is first white man
        known to set foot on slopes of Mount
        McKinley. First auto arrives at South Rim
        of Grand Canyon.

1903   President Theodore Roosevelt visits Grand
        Canyon.

1904   Bill to establish Elk National Park in
        Olympics fails.

1905   Paunsaugunt Plateau in Bryce Canyon set
        aside as a national forest.

1906   Mesa Verde National Park established. Idea

to make Hawaii Volcanoes area a park pro-
moted. Petrified Forest named a national
monument.

1906-08 Charles Sheldon, noted hunter-naturalist,
        visits Mount McKinley to study Dall sheep
        and other wildlife; becomes proponent of
        preserving area.

1907   Cinder Cone and Lassen Peak named na-
        tional monuments.

1908   President Theodore Roosevelt establishes
        Grand Canyon National Monument. First
        ranger-guided trips conducted to Mesa
        Verde's Cliff Dwellings: Spruce Tree House
        excavated by Dr. Jesse Walter Fewkes.

1909   Dr. Fewkes excavates Cliff Palace. President
        proclaims Mukuntuweap National Monu-
        ment. Mount Olympus National Monument,
        615,000 acreas, established.

1910

1910   Glacier National Park established. Automo-
        bile makes trips to Rockies practicable. First
        ascent of north peak of Mount McKinley
        (19,470 ft.) by Alaska sourdoughs.

1912   American scientist Thomas Jagger and
        others set up Hawaiian Volcano Research
        Association with an observatory on Mount
        Kilauea.

1915   Mount Rainier National Park established.
        Mount Lassen erupts. 124 Congressmen
        visit Hawaii to investigate possibilities for a
        national park. Rocky Mountain National
        Park established. After war, tourist boom
        in national parks.

1915-22 Dr. Fewkes excavates several cliff dwell-
        ings and mesa-top sites in the Mesa Verde.

1916   Lassen Volcanic National Park established.
        Hawaii National Park established. National
        Park Service created.

1917   Mount McKinley National Park established.
        Beginning of the 11-year administration of
        Steven T. Mather as NPS Director. Mather
        sought to make parks known to more per-
        sons, build park museums, preserve natural
        aspects; helped establish 12 national parks.

1918   Explorations by LeRoy Jeffers in Bryce Can-
        yon publicize area. Mukuntuweap National
        Monument enlarged and name changed to
        Zion. Park service ranger force replaces
        soldiers in national parks.

1919   Grand Canyon National Park established.
        Zion National Park established. Utah legisla-
        ture proposes to Congress that Bryce Canyon
        be made a national park.

1920

1920   Campfire lecture series and nature study
        trips instituted in Yosemite.

1922   43,000 acres, mainly the Kau Lava Flow in
        the Kau Desert, added to Hawaii National
        Park.

1923   Bryce Canyon National Monument established. Wagon road to Savage River Camp near Mount McKinley completed; Alaska Railroad completed. Explorations of Carlsbad Caverns by James Larkin White included in report by Robert Holley of the General Land Office, United States Department of Interior. Carlsbad Cave National Monument authorized.

1923-24 Exploration of Carlsbad Caverns by Dr. Willis T. Lee conducted by and reported by National Geographic Society.

1924 Bryce Canyon National Park authorized. Kilauea erupts; steam blast ends the lava lake phase in Halemaumau. Archaeological surveys, excavations begin in the Mesa Verde.

1926 Mauna Loa eruption destroys Hoopuloa.

1928 Bryce Canyon National Park established.

1929 Grand Teton National Park established. Beginning of 4-year administration of Horace M. Albright as Director, NPS. Previously Mather's assistant, Albright saw many important roads built providing access to parks: Zion-Mt. Carmel, Wawona Tunnel and Road, Grand Canyon Cape Royal Road, Paradise Valley, Yakima Park Hwy., and new road across divide in Rocky Mountains, among many. Three new parks added.

1930

1930 Carlsbad Caverns National Park established.

1932 Waterton-Glacier International Peace Park established.

1933 President Hoover proclaims additional 9,239 acres in Carlsbad Caverns National Park. Beginning of 7-year administration of Arno B. Cammerer as Director, NPS. He oversees complete study to get a plan for adequate park facilities. CCC does much park work during Depression era. Winter use of parks increases.

1935 Efforts renewed for an Olympic National Park.

1936 NPS gets Congress to provide for adequate water rights.

1937 Second Zion National Monument established. President Franklin Roosevelt visits Olympic Peninsula. Rocky Mountain irrigation tunnel authorized and begun despite opposition of NPS, NP Assn., and conservationists.

1938 Olympic National Park established. Mount McKinley park road built.

1939 President Roosevelt adds 39,488 acres to Carlsbad Caverns National Park

1940

1940 Kings Canyon (encompassing General Grant National Park) established. Addition made to Olympic National Park. Beginning of 11-year administration of Newton B. Drury as Director, NPS. Educational-Interpretive branch of NPS grows.

1941 Park appropriations cut in half during World War II. National Parks Concessioners, Inc. formed.

1942 Lava flow from Mauna Loa comes within 12 miles of the city of Hilo.

1943 Jackson Hole National Monument established. Addition to Olympic National Park.

1945 War over; tourists head for the parks.

1947-50 Dam threats to parks by Bureau of Reclamation, Army Engineers.

1950

1950 Jackson Hole added to Grand Teton National Park. Mauna Loa's eruption destroys village.

1951 Secretary of Interior Oscar Chapman issues order barring Bureau of Reclamation from surveys and investigations in national parks and monuments, wilderness areas and wildlife areas. Beginning of administration of Conrad Wirth as Director, NPS. During this time greater freedom accorded park service, more private land acquired, ambitious Mission 66 plan conceived and adopted.

1952 Kilauea eruption lasts 136 days.

1953 Queets Corridor and Pacific Coast area added to Olympic National Park.

1954 Brilliant eruption of Kilauea lasts 4 days.

1955 Kilauea erupts again, lasts 55 days.

1956 Monument added to Zion National Park. Mission 66 project begun by NPS—a 10-year conservation and improvement program.

1957 Denali Highway completed to Mount McKinley.

1958 Archaeological survey and excavation in the Mesa Verde begun by the Wetherill Mesa Archaeological Project.

1959 Kilauea makes most spectacular eruption in its recorded history; fountains of molten lava 1,900 ft. high. Earthquake in Yellowstone destroys campground, creates new lake.

1960

1960 Kilauea's month-long eruption sends lava flowing to the sea; adds 500 acres.

1961 Haleakala section made separate national park. Original park name changed to Hawaii Volcanoes.

1962 Petrified Forest National Park established.

1964 Yosemite celebrates centennial of Abraham Lincoln's proclamation setting aside the Valley and Mariposa Grove as a park under state of California; Pioneer History Center dedicated. Canyonlands National Park is established.

1965 Opening of West Yellowstone airport.

1968 Redwood and North Cascades National parks established.

Bibliography

This bibliography is generally limited to books, pamphlets, and articles that are likely to be found in a large library or a good bookstore. In addition to the titles listed, there is a wealth of material published within each park by a non-profit association from which books, maps, films, and color slides may be ordered by mail. Addresses of these associations are listed on pages 274-275.

NATIONAL PARKS—GENERAL

Bolin, Luis A. *National Parks of the United States.* New York: Knopf, 1962.

Butcher, Deveraux. *Exploring Our National Parks and Monuments.* New York: Houghton Mifflin Co., 1956.

Fryxell, Fritiof (ed.). *Francois Matthes and the Marks of Time.* San Francisco: Sierra Club Books, 1962.

Haines, Madge and Leslie Morrill. *John Muir, Protector of the Wilds.* New York: Abingdon Press, 1957.

Harrison, A. E. *Exploring Glaciers—With a Camera.* San Francisco: Sierra Club Books, 1960.

Ise, John. *Our National Park Policy, A Critical History.* Baltimore: John Hopkins Press, 1961.

Laycock, George. *America's Endangered Wildlife.* New York: Norton.

Matthews, William H., III. *National Parks.* New York: Barnes and Noble, 1964.

Melbo, Irving H. *Our Country's National Parks.* 2 vols. New York: Bobbs-Merrill Co., Inc., 1963.

Muir, John. *The Mountains of California.* New York: Doubleday & Co., 1962.

———. *Our National Parks.* Boston: Houghton Mifflin Co., 1916.

National Geographic Society. *America's Wonderlands, The National Parks.* Washington, D.C.: National Geographic Society, 1959.

Palmer, Ralph S. *The Mammal Guide: Mammals of North America, North of Mexico.* New York: Doubleday & Co.

Preston, Richard J., Jr. *North American Trees.* Ames, Iowa: Iowa State University Press.

Schultz, G. *Glaciers and the Ice Age.* New York: Holt, Rinehart and Winston, 1963.

Sunset Magazine Editors, *California National Parks.* Menlo Park, Calif.: Lane Magazine & Book Co., 1969.

Teale, Edwin Way. *Wilderness World of John Muir.* New York: Houghton Mifflin Co., 1954.

Tilden, Freeman. *The National Parks, What They Mean to You and Me.* New York: Knopf, 1951.

Udall, Stewart L. & Country Beautiful Editors. *National Parks of America.* New York: Putnam, 1966.

Wood, Francis and Dorothy. *Animals in Danger.* New York: Dodd, Mead & Co.

Yaeger, Dorr. *Your Western National Parks.* New York: Dodd, Mead & Co., 1947.

BRYCE CANYON

Barnett, John. *Bryce Canyon National Park.* Bryce Canyon Natural History Association, 1964.

CANYONLANDS

Crampton, C. G. *Standing Up Country: The Canyonlands of Utah and Arizona.* New York: Knopf, 1964.

CARLSBAD CAVERNS

Lee, Willis T. "A Visit to Carlsbad Cavern," *National Geographic Magazine,* XLV No. 1 (1924), 1-40.

———. "New Discoveries in Carlsbad Cavern," *"National Geographic Magazine,* XLVIII No. 3 (1925), 301-320.

CRATER LAKE

Sharpe, Grant and Wenonah. *101 Wildflowers of Crater Lake National Park.* Seattle, Wash.: University of Washington Press, 1959.

Williams, Howel. *Crater Lake: The Story of its Origin.* Berkeley, Calif.: University of California Press, 1957.

GLACIER

Craighead, John F. and others. *A Field Guide to Rocky Mountain Wildflowers.* New York: Houghton Mifflin Co., 1963.

Edwards, Gordon J. *A Climber's Gyide to Glacier National Park.* San Francisco: Sierra Club Books, 1960.

Ruhle, George C. *Guide to Glacier National Park.* Minneapolis: John W. Forney, 1957.

Scharff, Robert. *Glacier National Park and Waterton Lakes National Park.* New York: Hastings House.

GRAND CANYON

Dellenbaugh, Frederick S. *Canyon Voyage.* New Haven: Yale University Press (rev. ed.), 1962.

Farquhar, Francis P. *Books of the Colorado River and the Grand Canyon, a Selective Bibliography.* Los Angeles: Dawson's, 1953.

Krutch, Joseph Wood. *Grand Canyon: Today and All its Yesterdays.* New York: Sloane, 1958.

———. *Grand Canyon.* New York: Doubleday.

Powell, John Wesley. *Exploration of the Colorado River.* Chicago: University of Chicago Press, 1957.

———. *Exploration of the Colorado River.* New York: Doubleday & Co. (Reprint of the 1895 report.)

Scharff, Robert. *Grand Canyon National Park.* New York: Hastings House.

Watkins, T. H. and others. *The Grand Colorado.* Palo Alto, Calif.: American West Publishing Co., 1969.

GRAND TETON

Bonney, Orrin and Lorraine G. *Teton Range Field Guide.* Denver, Colo.: Swallow Press.

———. *Bonney's Guide to Jackson's Hole and Grand Teton National Park.* Houston, Tex.: Bonney.

Carrighar, Sally. *One Day at Teton Marsh*. New York: Knopf, 1947.

Fryxell, Fritiof. *Tetons: Interpretations of a Mountain Landscape*. Berkeley, Calif.: University of California Press, 1953.

Harry, Bryan. *Teton Trails*. Moose, Wyo.: Grand Teton Natural History Association.

Love, J. D. and John C. Reed, Jr. *Creation of the Teton Landscape*. U.S. Geological Survey, 1968.

Mattes, Merrill J. *Colter's Hell and Jackson's Hole*. Moose, Wyo.: Grand Teton Natural History Association.

Ortenburger, Leigh. *A Climber's Guide to the Teton Range*. San Francisco: Sierra Club Books, 1965.

HAWAII VOLCANOES/HALEAKALA

Hubbard, Douglass. *Ferns of Hawaii National Park*. Hawaii: Hawaii Natural History Association.

Kuck, Loraine E. and Richard C. Tongg. *Hawaiian Flowers and Flowering Trees*. Rutland, Vt.: Charles E. Tuttle Co.

Macdonald, Gordon and Douglass Hubbard. *Volcanoes of the National Parks in Hawaii*. Hawaii: Hawaii Natural History Association, 1961.

Munro, George C. *Birds of Hawaii*. Rutland, Vt.: Charles E. Tuttle Co. (rev. ed.).

Ruhle, George C. *Haleakala Guide*. Hawaii: Hawaii Natural History Association.

LASSEN VOLCANIC

Loomis, Benjamin F. *Eruptions of Lassen Peak*. Mineral, Calif.: Loomis Museum Association, 1966.

Schulz, Paul E. *Geology of Lassen's Landscape*. Mineral, Calif.: Loomis Museum Association.

———. *Indians of Lassen Volcanic National Park*. Mineral, Calif.: Loomis Museum Association.

Smith, Gladys L. *Flowers of Lassen Volcanic National Park*. Mineral, Calif.: Loomis Museum Association.

MESA VERDE

Fewkes, J. W. "Antiquities of Mesa Verde National Park: Cliff Palace," *Bureau of American Ethnology Bulletin*, No. 51 (1911).

———. "Antiquities of Mesa Verde National Park: Spruce Tree House," *Bureau of American Ethnology Bulletin*, No. 41 (1909).

Watson, Don. *Cliff Dwellings of the Mesa Verde*. Mesa Verde National Park, Colo.: The Mesa Verde Association, 1950.

———. *Indians of the Mesa Verde*. Mesa Verde National Park, Colo.: Mesa Verde Museum Association.

MOUNT McKINLEY

Anderson, J. P. *Flora of Alaska and Parts of Adjacent Canada*. Ames, Iowa: Iowa State University Press, 1959.

Murie, Adolph. *A Naturalist in Alaska*. (American Nature Series, No. 302.) New York: Devin-Adair Co., 1961.

———. *Birds of Mount McKinley. A field handbook*. McKinley Park, Alaska: Mount McKinley Natural History Association, 1963.

———. *Mammals of Mount McKinley*. McKinley Park, Alaska: Mount McKinley Natural History Association, 1962.

Pearson, Grant H. and Philip Newill. *My Life of High Adventure*. Englewood Cliffs, N.J.: Prentice-Hall, Inc., 1962.

Sheldon, Charles. *The Wilderness of Denali*. New York: Charles Scribner's Sons, 1960.

MOUNT RAINIER

Brockman, C. Frank. *Flora of Mount Rainier National Park*. Washington, D.C.: U.S. Government Printing Office, 1947.

———. *Trees of Mount Rainier National Park*. Seattle, Wash.: University of Washington Press, 1949.

Fiske, Hopson, and Waters. *Geology of Mount Rainier*. U.S. Geological Survey Professional Paper 444, 1963.

Haines, Aubrey L. *Mountain Fever: Historic Conquests of Mount Rainier*. Portland, Ore.: Oregon Historical Society, 1962.

Jones, George Neville. *The Flowering Plants and Ferns of Mount Rainier*. Seattle, Wash.: University of Washington Press, 1960.

Kirk, Ruth. *Exploring Mount Rainier*. Seattle, Wash.: University of Washington Press, 1968.

Meany, Edmond S. *Mount Rainier, Record of Exploration*. Portland, Ore.: Binfords and Mort, 1916.

Schmoe, Floyd. *Year in Paradise, Chronicle of Mount Rainier and Paradise Valley*. Rutland, Vt.: Charles E. Tuttle Co., 1968.

Sharp, Robert P. *Glaciers*. University of Oregon Books, 1960.

Sharpe, Grant and Wenonah, *101 Wildflowers of Mount Rainier National Park*. Seattle, Wash.: University of Washington Press, 1957.

Spring, Manning, and Mueller. *50 Hikes in Mount Rainier National Park*. Mount Rainier Natural History Association, Craftsman Press, Inc., 1969.

NORTH CASCADES/OLYMPIC

Spring, Bob and Ira. *The North Cascades National Park*. Seattle, Wash.: Superior Publishing Co., 1969.

Danner, Wilbert R. *Geology of Olympic National Park*. Seattle, Wash.: University of Washington Press, 1955.

Kirk, Ruth. *Exploring the Olympic Peninsula*. Seattle, Wash.: University of Washington Press.

———. *The Olympic Seashore*. Port Angeles, Wash. Olympic Natural History Association, 1962.

Leissler, Frederick. *Roads and Trails of Olympic National Park*. Seattle, Wash.: University of Washington Press, 1957.

Sharpe, Grant and Wenonah. *101 Wildflowers of Olympic National Park*. Seattle, Wash.: University of Washington Press, 1957.

PETRIFIED FOREST

Ransom, Jay Ellis. *Petrified Forest Trails: Field Guide*. Mentone, Calif.: Gembrooks.

———. *Petrified Forest Trails: Guide to the Petrified Forest of America*. Spokane, Wash.: J. D. Simpson and Co., 1955.

ROCKY MOUNTAIN

Bird, Isabella L. *Lady's Life in the Rocky Mountains*. Norman, Okla.: Oklahoma University Press, 1960.

Cargo and Chisholm. *Outdoorsman's Guide to Rocky Mountain National Park*. Estes Park, Colo.: Rocky Mountain Nature History Association, 1968.

Clements, F. E. and E. S. *Rocky Mountain Flowers*. New York: Hafner Publishing Co.

Craighead, John J. and others. *Field Guide to Rocky Mountain Wildflowers*. Boston: Houghton Mifflin Co., 1963.

Mills, Enos A. *Rocky Mountain National Park*. New York: Doubleday & Co., 1931.

Nelson, Ruth Ashton. *Plants of Rocky Mountain National Park*. Estes Park, Colo.: Rocky Mountain Nature Association, 1969.

Packard, Fred Mallery. *Birds of Rocky Mountain National Park*. Estes Park, Colo.: Rocky Mountain Nature Association, 1950.

REDWOOD

Hyde, Philip and Francois Leydet. *The Last Redwoods*. San Francisco: Sierra Club Books, 1963.

Iacopi, Robert. *Redwood Country*. Menlo Park, Calif.: Lane Magazine & Book Co., 1969.

Kauffman, John M. and Anthony B. Stewart. "Giant Sequoias: Earth's Largest Living Things Draw Millions to California Parks." *National Geographic*. Aug., 1959.

McCloskey, Michael. "The Last Battle of the Redwoods," *The American West*, VI (1969), No. 5, pages 58-64.

SEQUOIA AND KINGS CANYON

Alcorn, Wayne B. *Discovering Cone Bearing Trees in Sequoia-Kings Canyon*. Three Rivers, Calif.: Sequoia Natural History Association, 1967.

Brower, David. *Going Light with Backpack or Burro*. San Francisco: Sierra Club Books, 1960.

Carrighar, Sally. *One Day on Beetle Rock*. New York: Knopf, 1955.

Fry, Walter and John R. White. *Big Trees*. Stanford, Calif.: Stanford University Press, 1959.

Gray, Fern. *And the Giants Were Named*. Three Rivers, Calif.: Sequoia Natural History Association.

Johnston, Hank. *They Felled the Redwoods*. Los Angeles: Trans-Anglo Books, 1966.

Matthes, Francois E. *Sequoia National Park—A Geological Album*, Berkeley, Calif.: University of California Press, 1950.

Rockwell, Jack A. and Stephen K. Stocking. *Wildflowers of Sequoia-Kings Canyon*. Three Rivers, Calif.: Sequoia Natural History Association, 1969.

Starr, Walter A., Jr. *Starr's Guide to the John Muir Trail and the High Sierra Region*. San Francisco: Sierra Club Books, 1959.

Strong, Douglass Hillman. *Trees or Timber? The Story of Sequoia and Kings Canyon National Parks*. Three Rivers, Calif.: Sequoia Natural History Association, 1968.

Sumner, Lowell, and Joseph S. Dixon. *Birds and Mammals of the Sierra Nevada: With Records from Sequoia and Kings Canyon National Parks*. Berkeley, Calif.: University of California Press, 1953.

Voge, Hervey. *A Climber's Guide to the High Sierra*. San Francisco: Sierra Club Books, 1956.

White, John R. and Samuel J. Pusateri. *Illustrated Guide, Sequoia and Kings Canyon National Parks*. Stanford, Calif.: Stanford University Press, 1952.

YELLOWSTONE

Bauer, C. Max. *Yellowstone—its Underworld*. Albuquerque, N. Mex.: University of New Mexico Press, 1962.

Beal, Merrill D. *The Story of Man in Yellowstone*. Yellowstone Library and Museum Association, 1960.

Bonney, Orrin H. and Lorraine. *Absaroka Range and Yellowstone Park Field Guide*. Denver, Colo.: A Swallow, 1963.

Chittendon, Hiram M. *Yellowstone National Park*. (Richard A. Bartlett, ed.). Norman, Okla.: University of Oklahoma Press, 1964.

Fisher, William A. *Yellowstone's Living Geology*. Yellowstone Library and Museum Association, 1960.

Haynes, J. E. *Haynes Guide: Yellowstone National Park*. Bozeman, Mont.: Haynes Studios Inc., 1964.

Marler, George D. *The Story of Old Faithful*. Yellowstone Library and Museum Association, 1969.

Mills, H. B. *Bugs, Birds, and Blizzards in the Yellowstone*. Ames, Iowa: Collegiate Press, 1937.

Randall, Leslie W. Gay. *Footprints along the Yellowstone*. San Antonio, Tex.: Naylor Co.

YOSEMITE

Adams, Ansel and Nancy Newhall. *Yosemite Valley* San Francisco: Sierra Club Books.

Adams, Ansel and Virginia. *Illustrated Guide to Yosemite*. San Francisco: Sierra Club Books, 1963.

Degnan, Laurence and Douglass Hubbard. *Yosemite Yarns*. Fresno, Calif.: Awani Press, 1961.

Johnston, Hank. *Short Line to Paradise; Story of Yosemite Valley Railroad*. Long Beach, Calif.: Trans-anglo Books, 1962.

———. *Railroads of the Yosemite Valley*. Long Beach, Calif.: Trans-anglo Books, 1963.

Matthes, Francois E. *Incomparable Valley: a Geologic Interpretation of the Yosemite* (Fritiof Fryzell, ed.). Berkeley, Calif.: University of California Press, 1956.

Muir, John. *The Yosemite*. New York: Doubleday & Co., 1962.

Paden, Irene and Margaret Schlightmann. *Big Oak Flat Road to Yosemite*. Yosemite, Calif.: Yosemite Natural History Association, 1959.

Russell, Carl P. *One Hundred Years in Yosemite*. Yosemite, Calif.: Yosemite Natural History Association, 1959.

Sargent, Shirley. *Galen Clark, Yosemite Guardian*. San Francisco: Sierra Club Books, 1964.

———. *Pioneers in Petticoats, Yosemite's Early Women, 1856-1900*. Yosemite, Calif.: Flying Spur Press, 1966.

Tressider, Mary Curry and Della Taylor Hoss. *Trees of Yosemite National Park*. Yosemite, Calif.: Yosemite Natural History Association, 1963.

ZION

Burt, Olive. *Cave of Shouting Silence*. New York: John Day Co., 1960.

Hagood, Allen. *This is Zion*. Zion Natural History Association, 1969.

Woodbury, A. *A History of Southern Utah and Its National Parks*. Utah Historical Quarterly, Nos. 3 and 4.

Index

MT. McKINLEY

BEAUTY, GRANDEUR ... USEFULNESS

THE WEST'S two-dozen national parks comprise three-fourths of the national parks in the country and cover an equal fraction of the 14,500,000 acres in the system (in the accompanying map, the parks as well as Alaska and the Hawaiian Islands are distorted both in scale and position). In the West are the country's largest parks — Yellowstone (2,222,000 acres) and Mount McKinley (1,939,000 acres) — and the oldest: Yellowstone (established in 1872), Yosemite, Sequoia, and Kings Canyon (all in 1890), and Mount Rainier (1899). In a summer month, Western parks will attract half the entire system's visitors and two-thirds of the overnight vacationers. For overnighters, the nation's most popular park is Yosemite. For casual drop-ins, the West's most visited is the Grand Teton.

HAWAIIAN ISLANDS

HALEAKALA

HAWAII
VOLCANOES